RESTORING THE SHAMED

Restoring the Shamed

Towards a Theology of Shame

⮑

ROBIN STOCKITT

CASCADE *Books* • Eugene, Oregon

RESTORING THE SHAMED
Towards a Theology of Shame

Cascade Books
A Division of Wipf and Stock Publishers
199 W. 8th Ave., Suite 3
Eugene, OR 97401

www.wipfandstock.com

ISBN 13: 978-1-61097-315-1

Cataloging-in-Publication data:

Stockitt, Robin.

Restoring the shamed : towards a theology of shame / Robin Stockitt.

x + 172 p. ; 23 cm. Includes bibliographical references.

ISBN 13: 978-1-61097-315-1

1. Shame. 2. Shame in the Bible. 3. Shame—Religious aspects—Christianity. I. Title.

BF575.S45 S70 2012

Manufactured in the U.S.A.

Contents

Foreword

IT IS NOT HARD to sense the passion in these pages. In much contemporary theology, we are offered a series of cool, take-it-or-leave-it musings. But that is not the tone of *Restoring the Shamed*. This is a passionate book, in all the right senses. First and foremost, there is Stockitt's passion to urge the reader to engage a theme much neglected by theologians: the reality of human shame. As he demonstrates clearly, this is a pervasive current in the biblical witness that cannot easily be accommodated within the traditional schemes of sin-guilt-forgiveness. We are led through a wide array of relevant scriptural passages, and made to re-read and re-think familiar texts. Stockitt shows us not only that shame assumes many forms and many masks, but also that its various guises call for many different modes of knowing to do them justice. So we are given not only detailed exegesis and doctrine, but an array of wisdom from other sources, including poetry, philosophy, and psychology.

Stockitt is also passionate about not letting the reader off the hook. There are topics tackled here that many of us would prefer to skate around, so fraught and convoluted are the issues surrounding them. But those of us who know Robin well will be familiar with the way he presses you to face awkward questions, stubbornly pushing you beyond the comfy answers we use to protect ourselves. And that is very much the style here. Justification, sin, punishment, wrath—no topic seems too hot to handle, no angular stone is left unturned.

But the passion is not angry or aggressive. Quite the opposite. As Stockitt himself acknowledges at the start, all theology emerges from a habitat, and the habitat in this case is a wealth of pastoral experience, from prison ministry to the leadership of a lively multi-cultural congregation. Here you will find passion laced with *com*passion. The pervading aroma is that of grace, the grace-ful restoring of our shamed lives through the healing power of the gospel.

The pastoral habitat also prevents Stockitt's theological passion from flying off into the air. Here is scholarly theology earthed in the contingencies and unpredictabilities of your life and mine—death and birth, sickness and health, tears and joy, mourning and celebrating. The academic and the everyday are seamlessly interwoven.

Perhaps most important, Stockitt's passion is evident in the emotional appeal of the writing—an appeal that never descends into emotionalism. The chapter on "The Face," for example, is hard to read without the "affections" (to use a term from an earlier age) being deeply stirred.

In short, reading this book will not only help restore the shamed. It will likely restore a godly passion—and few things are more sorely needed in theology today.

Jeremy S. Begbie
Thomas A. Langford Research Professor, Duke Divinity School

Acknowledgements

THIS STUDY INTO THE theology of shame began some fifteen years ago while I was studying at Ridley Hall Anglican Theological College, Cambridge. At that time I took a class in Christian Doctrine with Professor Jeremy Begbie and he invited us to compose our own essay title as the final assignment of his course. I chose to look at shame and the resultant essay was eventually published in the *Anvil Theological Journal* in the summer of 1998. After that, the subject lay dormant for me, as a theme for academic enquiry.

In the ensuing years of pastoral work, however, I began to notice that shame appeared to be a pervasive feature of human existence, manifesting itself in a range of ingenious guises. So when I engaged in some challenging conversations about the wrath of God with some young students a few years ago, I found myself drawn back to look again at my earlier essay. I decided it was time to bring the topic to the forefront of my thinking and the book you now hold is the outcome of that process.

Over the course of writing and researching I have become deeply indebted to a number of people who have offered me encouragement, support, and critical reflections. Professor Christoph Schwöbel of Tübingen University encouraged me to pursue my theological instincts and pointed me to the recent work of Professor Robert Jewett. My subsequent meeting with Professor Jewett in a cafe at Heidelberg railway station proved to be a great catalyst for further enquiry. I am grateful too for stimulating conversations with George Norwood and for the thoughtful and constructive comments of friends who read initial drafts of this book. They include Andrew Tweedy, Nick Clarke, Sharon Schauer, Michael Westerman, Petra Jauslin, Judith Moratscheck, Philip Geck, Katja Hildebrand, and Rt. Rev. Dr. Geoffrey Rowell. My editor at Cascade, Robin Parry, has been a friendly, approachable, and insightful critic. The congregation of the

Acknowledgements

Anglican Church in Freiburg, Germany, have, as usual, been the recipients of these ideas and have always allowed me generous space to think out loud. Lastly—and most significantly—my wife, Joan, has travelled with me on this path, offering endless hours of listening, encouraging, and loving.

PART 1

Entering Shame

1

Introduction

"Love bade me welcome; but my soul drew back"

ALL THEOLOGICAL ENQUIRY EMERGES from a habitat. That habitat is the environment in which ideas germinate, take root, and eventually blossom. At times the environment is adversarial, with proponents of one theory pitted against those of another. Across the span of Christian history it is not hard to find times when tension was high and much was at stake. One only has to think of the debates that raged over the divinity of Christ in the early centuries of the church, or the tensions surrounding the origin and purpose of the Holy Spirit in the eleventh century, or the controversy over the theme of "justification" that so consumed the reformers. What is perhaps less obvious is how the crucible of theological enquiry is also shaped by the intensity of the personal experiences of the theologian. The great Augustine, who continues to exert a profound influence on theology, was shaped by the recklessness of his youth, his own sense of guilt, his training in law, his spiritual awakening in a garden in Milan—all of these had their part to play in the subsequent emergence of his grandest theological insights.

The theological exploration in this book is no different. It has emerged from my own struggles to place together the genuine, authentic experiences of ordinary human beings with the mystery of the birth, the life, the ministry, the death, and the resurrection of Christ. It is an attempt to reflect on the experiences of life in the light of the biblical story of God's engagement with the world that he has made. My professional work has been divided into two halves; one in the world of education and the other as an ordained Anglican minister. As an educator, I worked primarily with those who experienced severe learning difficulties, with those whose behavior was profoundly challenging, and with those in prison. My work took me to the far corners of human experience including the poorest of the poor in rural Africa, inmates in prison with hair-raising criminal records, and ordinary young people struggling with the stresses and strains of modern living. In my present work as the pastor of a multi-cultural church with over twenty-five nationalities represented, I come into daily contact with people at all stages of life and in a dazzling collection of demanding situations. Over the years I have listened to countless stories depicting the joys and the traumas, the dreams and the disappointments, the abuses and the delights of being human.

Over the course of these years I have searched for resonances between my Christian faith and the people whom I have encountered. Is this troubled world essentially "good" as Gen 1 clearly proclaims, or profoundly "fallen" as Gen 3 suggests? Are the troubled people I have encountered over the years profound "sinners" or simply "glorious ruins," to borrow a phrase from C. S. Lewis? How can one depict and delineate the picture of humanity that surrounds us in a way that does justice to both the biblical testimony and the raw reality of being alive? In all of my experiences, even during my years working in a maximum security prison, I have never met anyone whom I would wish to describe as truly evil and intentionally malicious. Even though I have talked with those who have committed dreadful crimes and I have met wounded, abused, neglected men who have done wicked things to others, I would hesitate to call any of them "great sinners." Yet the language of sin and sinner is profoundly biblical, and that is precisely the problem. How do we place these two worlds side by side so that they touch each other? Where is the touching point, the tangent, where two horizons meet?

Let me tell you two stories involving people I have encountered. The first story involves one of the men I met while working in a prison as a teacher. He had achieved national notoriety as the most dangerous and evil person in Britain. I vividly recall teaching him elementary mathematics in the maximum security Special Unit. He was so notorious that the BBC had even made a television documentary about him, for his anger was so explosive that he had been known to kill prison officers with his bare hands. When I taught him he was unlocked from his prison cell by six fully armed and protected officers who then sat around the table as our lesson proceeded. In human terms he had plumbed the depths of human depravity and had forfeited his right to belong to society. In conversation with him, I learned that throughout his childhood he had been locked in a darkened cupboard by his abusive father. From time to time he was brought out and used by his father for target practice when using his air gun. The prisoner that sat in front of me had countless scars all over his body as grisly evidence of his traumatized childhood. By the time he reached adulthood prison psychologists had diagnosed him as having three distinct personalities. One was the polite and earnest adult with whom I could spend an enjoyable hour. The second was an infant who, from time to time, curled up into a fetal position and cried like a baby. The third was a raging monster, with superhuman strength able to overpower an armed guard with ease. How could we depict this man? Was he the ultimate example of evil, an illustration of the sinfulness of humankind? There is no doubt that he had committed grotesque crimes and caused immense grief and suffering to others. Yet there is also no doubt that his own traumatized childhood, the place of persistent and brutal humiliation, had contributed to the development of his split personality and his violent behavior. It was as if his experience of being thoroughly humiliated contributed, with tragic inevitability, to his later crimes. Here was a man who undoubtedly was thoroughly "guilty" in every sense of the word. Yet as I sat before him and looked into his eyes I began to feel that his deepest malaise was perhaps not guilt at all.

The second story involves a woman who, in early adulthood, developed a friendship with a man. As their relationship evolved over time, the man began to display increasingly violent behavior towards her, culminating in repeated acts of sexual violence. These experiences left her feeling deeply traumatized and ashamed. She was an innocent victim of crimes committed against her, yet despite being innocent, she experienced an enduring and deep sense of pollution. On learning of her story I was compelled to reflect on how the incarnation of Christ and his redeeming work could touch the life of a human being so deeply scarred. This woman tells her own story in the final chapter of this book.

The atoning work of Christ is often defined and depicted in terms of the need to deal with the overwhelming problem of the universal sinfulness and guilt of humanity, which requires urgent attention by God. There is no question that our world is a broken and distorted place, tainted by a disease that permeates all that there is. Yet it is also a place of great beauty and order, with countless daily examples of acts of generosity and kindness. Where, then, is the point of contact between the biblical worldview that all of creation is desperately in need of redemption and the world that we all experience, which contains a confusing mixture of hope and despair, fear and courage, selflessness and greed? What is it about our world that is so profoundly damaged that God chose to come in person, in Jesus, to restore it and make it new? The trouble is that the world of our own experience and the world of the Bible do not easily connect with each other. There is often little resonance between the biblical depiction of ancient peoples in a distant land and modern present-day existence. Most people simply do not recognize themselves in the mirror that announces their "great sin," and therefore the cross of Christ is rendered meaningless at best or repugnant at worst. The problem therefore is one of a lack of connection.

Yet I have met many people, hundreds, even thousands of people, who do experience something more profound than the rather straightforward sin-guilt-forgiveness paradigm of traditional Christian orthodoxy. It is far more difficult to define but afflicts us all in a pervasive way. It is the nagging feeling that maybe we are not quite good enough, that we are insignificant, that we have not made our mark on the world. In more severe cases it expresses itself in the driving need to perform, to compete against others for the right to exist. Or it is manifested in the desire to hide, to withdraw, to retreat into some safer world where no one can hurt or destroy. This malaise sometimes erupts in violence done to others for no apparent reason, or it smolders beneath the surface eating away at our self-esteem and our bodies. For some it is camouflaged by an excess of pious spirituality; for others by a weary resignation. We go to extraordinary lengths to run away from this disease of the soul, by denying it is there, by refusing to stop, by filling every corner of our lives with busyness, hoping that the dread feeling will simply drift away and disappear.

What is the name of this experience?

It is called shame.

It may masquerade, however, under a variety of different pseud-onyms: Disgrace, ridicule, humiliation, unworthiness, contempt, con-demnation—to name but a few. I intend to collect this cluster of names together under one heading, the title of *shame*. If this shame is so per-vasive, so universally evident, then surely we require a theology to un-derstand it and to address it. That is the purpose of this book, to attempt to build a bridge across the chasm between our experience of being hu-man in a wonderful yet tragic world and the real events that took place in Jerusalem just a little over two thousand years ago. The investigation will look at the way in which shame is without doubt a socially constructed phenomenon, with profoundly personal, spiritual and political repercus-sions. It has been the subject of anthropological and psychological en-quiry for some time. Yet I believe it is more than any of these: there is a *theological* dimension to shame that speaks to our very being, our own anthropology. To my knowledge, very little theological exploration has yet been undertaken on this theme.

It may be possible to raise an early objection here. Is shame nothing more than a human construction? Is it simply the product of our twisted relationships within society, which has significant implications for the way in which we organize ourselves but possesses no intrinsic theological value? If this is true, can we therefore claim that shame is a valid theo-logical category—along with guilt—occupying a central position in the diagnosis of the human predicament that the Bible refers to as "sin"? The question presupposes, however, that the boundary line between our sta-tus before God as human beings and the status of our ordinary, everyday human relationships can be clearly demarcated. It is my contention that this is a false distinction. We know who we are both in the way in which we relate to our Creator and the way in which we live with our neighbor. The two together constitute our anthropology. The Genesis account of creation, which we will explore in due course, functions theologically in much the same way as embryonic stem cells in the human body. From the first division of cells immediately after conception the DNA of these cells determine the future growth of the body into an adult. They are capable of development and transformation into a vast range of other human tissue. The Genesis scriptures act, therefore, as our foundational text in which we see humankind standing before God in the context of a garden, with a real job to do that requires getting one's hands dirty. There are plants that need tending, animals that require care, and food that has to be gathered and prepared. It is an image of human society lived within the loving orbit of God's care. It is the description of community, both human and divine, which taken together depicts our identity. We know who we are in the very ordinariness of human existence precisely because that is where God chooses to make himself known. If that ordinary place becomes tainted with shame, then it is a distortion that infects every aspect of who we are, our sense of self, our relationship with God, and our connectedness to our neighbor.

The approach that I take in this investigation is a speculative one. Our theology in the Western tradition has become accustomed to a particular paradigm that begins with the pressing need to address the problem of human guilt before God, and it is from this starting point that a theological edifice has been constructed. What happens to this construction if we begin somewhere else? How does the message of the creating and redeeming love of God look if the human predicament is defined differently? What happens to our theology if "shame" is the name of the disease that has entered our world? This is where the speculation lies, in proposing an alternative diagnosis and allowing that diagnosis to determine how the healing and restoring work of God in Christ is offered.

Images of the cross of Christ are the inspiration for countless thousands of works of art across the centuries and across the globe. This one event has inspired the astonishing Isenheim altarpiece in Colmar, Bach's Passions, and innumerable other powerful artistic interpretations. Yet despite this, the cross remains a profound mystery. Out of the many crucifixions that took place during the period of Roman dominance, this one death alone stands out as being worthy of remembrance. This one event overflows with such a surplus of meaning that even after two thousand years we have yet to exhaust its interpretation. Much of the history of this interpretation revolves around understanding the nature of the "exchange" that apparently took place on that first Easter. Something momentous happened, so we are told, between humanity and God—or indeed between the whole cosmos and God—that means that the subsequent unfolding of human history has never been the same. And this exchange has often been framed in terms of some key concepts—sin, guilt, justice, forgiveness. This book will explore all of these in due course, but not, I hasten to add, in an abstract way. The Bible is offered to us not as a collection of philosophical theories, ideas that we must somehow drag from "up there" into our confused, joyful, tragic, and wonderful lives. Rather the Bible is a library of stories that fit together to tell one big story, the story of the heartbeat of God for the world that he has made. Any attempt to make sense of the cross of Christ, therefore, must begin and end with biblical stories, peppered with poetry and wisdom that together, as a whole, help us understand the theology, the meaning of events that involved real people and a real God.

Fitting the stories together is no easy task. It is akin to the childhood pastime of joining up the dots to create a picture. How one joins the dots demands creativity, integrity, and imagination, and the final picture requires interpretation before it will reveal its meaning. The well-known French philosopher Paul Ricoeur referred to this process as "configuring the narrative." By this he meant that all of human life is composed of stories—narratives—that need to be connected together in order to find meaning. How one connects the stories together is the process of configuration, knowing the order and the emphasis needed to establish some kind of coherence, thereby leading to a meaningful interpretation. It may be that there are many ways of configuring the different stories, produced over millennia in distant and foreign cultures. We are left with no option, however, but to make an attempt at this configuration, and my guiding principle is quite simple: it is the big story about the heartbeat of God's love; a God who comes looking for his lost, guilty, and shamed people.

This book will attempt to address this one forgotten, ignored, overlooked aspect of many of the stories of the Bible, turning around the crucial questions of how honor often turns into shame and how shame, as a result of the initiative of God, can be redeemed and healed. I suspect that this has become the orphan of Western theology because of the huge cultural distance between our own world and the ancient world of the Near East. Our Western world, out of which so much theological reflection has emerged, is a very different place from ancient Near East at the time of Abraham, Isaac, and Jacob. Our culture—influenced, as it has been so heavily, by Greek concepts of abstract thought and in recent centuries by a more rampant individualism—is a world away from the time when extended families lived and worked the land and travelled across desert landscapes in response to the call of the God they named Yahweh. Yet there are many places in the world to this day that are closer to biblical culture, where the concepts of honor and shame are the driving forces behind many traditions and inform the way in which relationships are pursued.

So I make no apologies for beginning with a poem that is not even from the Bible, yet which captures the essence of what this book will seek to explore.

Love (poem 286)

Love bade me welcome; yet my soul drew back,
    Guilty of dust and sin.
But quick-ey'd Love, observing me grow slack
    From my first entrance in,
Drew nearer to me, sweetly questioning,
    If I lack'd anything.

"A guest," I answer'd, "worthy to be here":
    Love said, "You shall be he."
"I, the unkind, ungrateful? Ah, my dear,
    I cannot look on Thee."
Love took my hand and smiling did reply,
    "Who made the eyes but I?"

"Truth Lord; but I have marred them: Let my shame
    Go where it doth deserve."
"And know you not," says Love, "who bore the blame?"
    "My dear, then I will serve."
"You must sit down," says Love, "and taste my meat."
    So I did sit and eat.

George Herbert (1593–1632), the famous seventeenth-century poet, penned these poignant lines and in so doing illuminated this most *dominant yet hidden experience* of humankind. The claim that shame is both dominant and hidden is a bold one, yet one that I am convinced is profoundly true. In Herbert's poem the one who is praying feels compelled to withdraw and hide from the pursuit of love. How is it possible to stand in the presence of grace with head held high and arms outstretched in welcome when one feels too small, too insignificant and polluted even to draw breath? Better to turn and run in the opposite direction away from those all seeing, all knowing eyes that behold one's inner being with irresistible love. This is the heart of shame, the awful dread that tells us we don't belong, that we don't deserve anything, and that we shouldn't even *be*.

I am persuaded, therefore, that an understanding of shame will shed critical new light on the ministry of Jesus Christ, culminating in his death on a cross. "God so loved the world," John tells us, "that he gave his one and only Son for us." Such a dramatic, daring intervention into our lives must have been necessitated by the dramatic, tragic violence that distorts the beautiful world that God created. But precisely what is the nature of this distortion? How is it to be described, defined, given form and shape? Unless this initial mapping of the problem is done, then the solution offered and accomplished by Christ makes little sense. Therefore, right at the outset of this investigation, we need to offer some idea, a sketch at least, of the theological architecture of shame. This will be our first task.

2

Architecture

WHAT DOES SHAME LOOK like? What is its design, structure, and purpose? How does it function in both ordering and distorting our world? These are questions that demand to be heard and point us in the direction of the foundational creation texts in the book of Genesis, which articulate a view of what it means to be human. Our search therefore is for a biblical anthropology, in which shame and its natural counterpart—honor—have a pre-eminent place.

The story begins starkly with the simple sentence, "In the beginning God created the heavens and the earth." It is the story of God, who chooses to create, to shape, to form, to urge, to advise, to persuade, and to woo the people that he made to inhabit and tend his extraordinarily wonderful creation. As the story unfolds we are given hints, clues, suggestions as to who this God is who steps onto the surface of our world and into the very heart of our lives. One of the first clues comes very quickly—"and the Spirit of God was hovering." God, who has just been introduced as the Creator of the heavens and the earth, is now also described as Spirit; a Spirit that "hovers" or "flutters" over the chaos and soon gets busy, separating light from dark, wet from dry, above from below. This God does his creating much as an artist would, by organizing, shaping, and giving boundaries and edges to the raw material at his disposal. And he does not do this as a single entity. The Spirit is active and so is God—who by the voice of his command brings creation into being—so it is perhaps no surprise that soon the storyteller drops another hint by telling us, "then God said, 'Let us make . . .'" So God is plural and yet somehow, mysteriously, we are *not* left with the impression that this is a plurality of gods working in committee. This is *one* God, but a God who is more than one. Our final clue, drawn from these opening three chapters is offered after the creation of humankind, when we read the intriguing phrase, "the sound of the LORD God as he was walking in the garden in the cool of the day." What is the storyteller trying to communicate here? A God who throws the stars into space, who can separate light from dark, yet who also walks in the garden in the cool of the day. This God becomes more fascinating and yet more mysterious as the narrative progresses. God is transcendent, entirely "other," separate and distinct from the rest of creation; yet simultaneously he is also profoundly near, immanent, the God who is depicted in incarnational terms walking in a garden, searching for a conversation partner. Placing all these pieces of evidence together we are drawn to the conclusion that the storyteller is urging us to view God as a community of persons, intimately involved in every aspect of his creation.

If this is the God with whom we have to do, then he becomes the arbiter, the criterion against which we can measure the true stature of ourselves as human beings. Right from the outset we are given indications that God functions relationally to both himself and to the world he has just brought into being. These hints become stronger and more pronounced as the narrative unfolds such that by the time Jesus appears in public for the very first time on the banks of the river Jordan, before an eccentric prophet and a bewildered crowd, we are given the fullest expression of that divine community of persons. When the writer of Genesis tells us that we are made in the image of this divine community, he is telling us something critically important for our own self-understanding. A part of what it means to bear God's likeness is that human beings are *intrinsically relational*. This is the way that we are constituted; this forms the heart of who we are and what it is to be fully human. In this initial quest to define the nature of shame it is necessary, therefore, to anticipate that it will have a distorting effect on this essential communal aspect of who we are. If shame is a dimension of the sin that has made such an unwelcome entry into creation, then it follows that it must possess an essentially corporate and relational dimension. The state of "sin" carries with it a sense of being out of relationship in some profound way, where the sense of belonging to a community is ruptured.

However, the creation stories in Genesis are not the only ones that the Bible offers. The wisdom tradition—located in the books of Job, Proverbs, Ecclesiastes, and the Song of Solomon—is a rich treasury of creation theology. Proverbs 8 proclaims in wonderful poetic imagery the delight with which Wisdom, depicted in female terms, stood by God's side at the moment of creation, rejoicing in all that was being brought forth. "Then I was the craftsman at his side. I was filled with delight day after day, rejoicing always in his presence, rejoicing in his whole world and delighting in mankind" (Prov 8:30–31). The text of Prov 8 bears witness to a distinct tradition in the history of Israel's testimony to the true nature of Yahweh. Here we read of the manner in which the world was brought into being, via the agency of Wisdom. When God created the world, Wisdom was by his side as the architect, the master craftsman, even the nursemaid of this creative process.[1] The prevailing characteristics of this Wisdom are described as delight and playfulness. Wisdom plays before the face of, or in the presence of, God—a highly suggestive theatrical image, with Wisdom as the actor, playing for and delighting in God who enjoys the performance. The wisdom tradition thus depicts creation in a dramatic and intensely loving manner. The entire portrayal is filled with a sense of delight and appreciation both for the Creator and for creation itself. The American theologian David Kelsey has this to say about God's creative actions: "How shall we characterize the triune Creator's active relating to creation? . . . This is the ultimate context in which we are born. God's hospitable generosity, creatively relating, to us, and attentively delighting in us."[2]

Knowing Ourselves in the Face of Another

If we hold together the wisdom tradition and the Genesis accounts of creation what picture emerges? As humans we are born into a world that is intrinsically communal and whose hallmark is one of playful delight. This is our true home and when we are able to live with heads held high, caring

1. The Hebrew term in Prov 8:30 can be rendered in a variety of possible meanings intended to convey the sense of either "caring for" or "constructing."

2. Kelsey, *Eccentric Existence*, 175.

for creation, delighting, frolicking and playing with others and with our Creator, it is then that we know who we are. It is a depiction of the architecture of the self that is composed of a set of relationships that together hold humanity in creative tension, much as a spider's web is anchored in a number of places and its interwoven strands give strength to the entire structure. We cannot know ourselves as islands detached and untouched by anyone else. We find out who we are in the face of another.

In the second chapter of Genesis the Lord declares that it is not good for Adam to remain alone (Gen 2:18). It is a statement declaring that for the human self to be fully realized there needs to be the presence of "another," for without this "other" we cannot know ourselves and are unable to flourish. This "other" in the case of Adam and Eve was similar and yet dissimilar. Adam recognizes that this person is of the same raw material as he himself—bone of my bones and flesh of my flesh—yet she is also utterly different. A partner, a companion, a counterpart, a complementary person, but certainly not a competitor. Without having each other Adam and Eve would not have been complete. This depiction is a theological assertion of the structure of the self. The DNA of who we are as persons is intrinsically relational and we are offered the merest glimpse into this state of innocence. Prior to the temptation by the serpent described in chapter 3, the storyteller informs us in Gen 2:25 that "the man and his wife were both naked, *and they felt no shame.*" What is the theological significance of this piece of information? Is this an incidental morsel of trivia about nudity? Can it be passed over without further attention? It is my view that this highly crafted story of creation includes significant clues that are essential to a correct configuration of the meaning of the narrative, and this reference is pivotal to unlocking the meaning of the tale. Before they choose to disobey the divine injunction Adam and Eve are described as being without shame. The Hebrew word here, *bôsh*, is used in such a way as to articulate that "the man and his wife were not found in a state of shame as far as their nakedness was concerned."[3] Indeed the verbal forms used in the Hebrew suggest that Adam and Eve *presented themselves* (a reflexive verb) as being without shame before each other. In other words they stood before each other, and before the God who created them, without covering, and felt no diminution of themselves and with no desire to hide. *Bôsh* is a Hebrew word that is found repeatedly

3. Botterwick and Rinngren, *Theological Dictionary of the Old Testament*, 52.

in the Old Testament—128 times to be precise—which suggests that it plays a significant role in the unfolding story of God's people. Here is a sinless world, a paradise, and the *primary characteristic*, as far as the first couple were concerned, was *the absence of shame*. This ancient account is a depiction of the human condition in a pre-cultural environment. Later we will observe how shame and its counterpart, honor, became embedded in the culture of what we now know as the Middle East and the Mediterranean rim. The Adam and Eve account speaks of a time before any kind of socially constructed understanding of shame. It would suggest that shamelessness is an original, existential description of who we are. Despite the absence of cultural moorings in the Gen 2 account, it nevertheless remains profoundly relational, for Adam and Eve recognized their own nakedness, the nakedness of another standing before them, and the entire story unfolds within the orbit of the utter "otherness" of God's creative care and knowledge.

This biblical structure of the human self finds an echo in the writings of the philosopher and theologian Paul Ricoeur, who spent a lifetime deliberating on the nature of human identity and the construction of the self. In his book *Oneself as Another*, he insists that there are three forms of "otherness" towards which each of us is impelled. It is through the dynamic interplay between these significant "others" that we know *we* are. The first of these three types of "other" is our relationship with ourselves, and most significantly with our bodies. Ricoeur claims that we are constantly in touch with the world around us through the very physicality of our being. We have five senses through which the world is presented to us. Our bodies are the conduit of information about our environment, the context in which we live and move and breathe and have our being. Our primary relationship therefore is with this body that we each possess. Those who have observed infants developing in the first months of life will know that one of their essential tasks is to learn to make the distinction between their own and the body of their mother.

The second form of "other" is the otherness of other people. When another person stands before me in relationship there is both sameness and difference. We recognize in the face of another the responsiveness of another human being. This person is affected by what I say and do, and in like manner I am affected by my own interaction with this significant "other." In one direction from myself to the other there is the recognition of the existence and legitimacy of another person who is not me. In the other direction, from the other to the self, there is the call to ethical behavior. Because there is an other person facing me, I cannot live solely in a relationship with myself—I am obliged to engage in moral, ethical choices because of the demand that this other makes upon me. There is a reciprocity between two people even if it is not always symmetrical or equal. This is how Ricoeur expresses his concept of *the self*: "The selfhood of oneself implies otherness to such an intimate degree that one cannot be thought of without the other."[4] The converse of this process of recognition is the path towards shame. When we, as persons designed and created to live in community, no longer recognize the presence of "another" as a gift from God, then division has entered the scene. The great German theologian Dietrich Bonhoeffer, who so courageously stood against the tyranny of Hitler's Third Reich, had this to say about Adam, Eve, and shame.

> Shame only exists as a result of the knowledge of the division of man . . . Shame is the expression of the fact that we no longer accept the other person as a gift from God . . . When one accepts the other as the companion given to him by God, where he is content with understanding himself as beginning from and ending in the other and in belonging to him, man is not ashamed. In the unity of unbroken obedience man is naked in the presence of man, uncovered, revealing both body and soul, and yet is not ashamed. Shame only comes into existence in the world of division.[5]

The third and final form of "otherness" is our relationship with "the wholly Other." There is always the possibility and indeed the necessity to go beyond what is tangible and verifiable. Another realm beckons us, a place of awe and beauty—the place, in fact, where God is found. This "wholly Other"—who is neither equal to us nor of the same raw material—invites us to be in relationship, providing us with the third leg of a triad of relationships holding the human self in healthy balance.

What happens, then, when one of these three fundamental relationships endures a rupture, a distortion of some kind? What effect does that have on the self and the sense of being a person? The picture of "naive" innocence presented in Gen 2 was fatally ruptured in Gen 3 when the original pair chose an alternative orientation. They heard the voice of the

4. Ricoeur, *Oneself as Another*, 3.
5. Bonhoeffer, *Creation and Fall*, 63.

serpent and their heads turned to listen to what the serpent had to say. The journey towards the breaking of the command began with the turning of their heads away from their Creator. The act of disobedience was the consequence of this turning away, the logical outcome of facing away from the divine community. It was this turning away that was indicative of a desire to sever the relationship of loving dependency upon God. To remain in relationship meant an acknowledgment of the giftedness of life and the origin of that gift in the God who had created them. The temptation to be as gods threatened that dependent connection and struck at the heart of what it was to be human.

Shame and Division

The immediate consequence of the turning away was the sudden entrance of shame. It announced its arrival with a new ability to "know," and this "knowing" produced an urgent desire to *hide*. When God finds the couple crouching behind a tree, they are too ashamed to come out into the open, for their shame is overwhelming (Gen 3:8–11). This is the storyteller's way of describing the experience of sin. Ultimately, this leads to expulsion from the garden, with no more evening conversations with the God who used to come looking for them. The resultant scenario, described so vividly in Gen 3:9–24, is heartbreaking in its tragic depiction. The man and woman experience a rupture of their own trusting relationship with each other; there is a sense of aloneness as both the man and woman face their separate challenges of toil and childbirth and there is no longer a harmony between them and creation. Above all they experience exclusion, they no longer belong, they become outsiders, and were it not for the provision of warm leather coats made through God's own tailoring, their darkness would have been complete. Undoubtedly there is true guilt depicted here. They were specifically asked to choose to remain in relationship with their Creator. The touchstone of that choice was the avoidance of one particular tree, which symbolized their own finite, created humanity as distinct from the uncreated life of God. In the making of their choice they incurred guilt and felt that guilt acutely. Yet the guilt that they jointly shared was merely one aspect of the larger story of their turning away, which culminated in their shameful expulsion from the place of true community and harmony with the whole of the created world. Bonhoeffer articulates the narrative in this way: "Man perceives himself in his disunion with God and men. He perceives that he is naked . . . laid bare. Hence there arises shame. Shame is man's ineffaceable recollection of his estrangement from the origin . . . man is ashamed of the loss of his unity with God and with other men. Shame and remorse are generally mistaken for one another. Man feels remorse when he has been at fault, and he feels shame when he lacks something. Shame is more original than remorse."[6]

Bonhoeffer acknowledges that both shame and remorse are present in the Genesis account. Remorse is the human response to the acknowledgment of guilt, and as such it is directly connected to a specific misdeed. Shame is far deeper than that—more "original," to use Bonhoeffer's description—and is often unconnected to specific acts of commission or omission. That original experience resonates with something that lies very deep within the human soul. It is the sense that something is essentially damaged, distorted, infected at the core of our being. It questions our very right to exist before the God who called us into being. The original memory is that we are made for unity and harmony, and shame reminds us of the disunity that now exists. The desire of Adam and Eve to cover their nakedness by making for themselves aprons, is a sign of their desire to cover that lack of original union. What began for them as the delight of daily open communion with the creator now manifests itself as terrified concealment. This is the awful dilemma that shame presents to us, the pendulum that continually swings back and forth between these two poles. Let us hear the words of Bonhoeffer again: "The dialectic of concealment and exposure is only a sign of shame. Shame can be overcome only when the original unity is restored, . . . shame is overcome only in the enduring of an act of final shaming, namely the becoming manifest of knowledge before God."[7]

Why linger on this ancient story? We do so for a number of reasons. Firstly, this is not so much a dictionary definition of sin presented as some kind of theological abstraction. Rather sin is defined in terms of a *story* that unfolds, and its characteristics and effects have both a shame and a guilt dimension. The shame of being excluded and finding oneself alone in the wide expanse of creation, without the reassuring, soothing voice of the Lord at the conclusion of each day, is a far deeper and more serious

6. Bonhoeffer, *Ethics*, 20.

7. Ibid., 22–23.

problem than the feeling of guilt for having broken a rule. It is not so much the rule breaking that is at issue; rather it is the altered orientation, the facing away from a community of grace, that is so shocking. The notion of facing away in Gen 3:8 is captured poignantly in the original Hebrew, but lost altogether in the English translation, which renders the verse, "they hid from the LORD God among the trees of the garden."[8] The Hebrew text depicts the couple as withdrawing away from the *face* (*pānîm*) of God. In the acuteness of their shame, their instinct was to turn immediately away from God's face. Here we observe the beginnings of a pattern of paired experiences; innocence, sinlessness, joy, and delight dwell together with an unashamed enjoyment in the face of God. By contrast, shame, guilt, and sin appear to be the natural consequences of a withdrawal from God's face.

These twin pairings appear repeatedly in the biblical narrative and two examples here will suffice to illustrate this pattern. The first comes from Gen 4, at the conclusion of the tragic story of Cain and Abel. Both brothers bring an offering of gratitude to God, but God's response is one of acceptance towards Abel but not towards Cain. The anger that this elicited from Cain was written all over his face. The writer describes his *pānîm* as "falling" (Gen 4:5). God notices that his face has fallen and responds by saying to him, "If you do what is right, will you not be accepted?" (Gen 4:7). The word that has been translated as "accepted" (*nāśā*ʾ) literally means "lifted up" so we could translate God's words as, "If you do what is right, will you not be *lifted up*?" This is a clear reference back to his fallen face. If he seeks restoration with God and overcomes the temptation towards bitter revenge, the result will be seen all over his uplifted face. Tragically, Cain is unable to come to terms with the jealous disappointment that lurks within him. Soon afterwards he kills his brother in a fit of rage and as a result has to face the consequences of his dreadful deed. His banishment from society excludes him, shamefully, from any possibility of belonging, and Cain realizes at once that such banishment will mean a painful withdrawal from the *pānîm* of God (Gen 4:14–16).

By contrast, dwelling before the face of God and enjoying his steady gaze upon our lives is the epitome of blessedness. One may witness the huge theological significance of this "orientation" in the well-known Aaronic blessing in Num 6:24–26: "The LORD bless you and keep you; the

---

8. New International Version.

LORD make his face shine upon you and be gracious to you; the LORD turn his face towards you and give you peace." Here Moses instructs Aaron to pronounce the blessing of God upon the wandering, fledgling nation of Israel in one profound image—the Lord's face is turned towards you. The knowledge that God was orienting his "face" towards his people was information enough to give renewed hope, strengthened determination, and firmer trust. For the Israelites, the knowledge that they lived beneath the gaze of God produced an enduring sense of safety and shameless intimacy. The Aaronic blessing is the antithesis of the expulsion of Adam and Eve from the garden. There God turned his face away in response to humankind's prior turning away. Out in the enervating wasteland of the desert God declares that despite the grumbling, stuttering faith of his people, they are held in the place of honor. Why then would Adam and Eve exchange shamelessness and relationship for shame and exclusion? It is almost beyond comprehension, yet that is the reality of the depth of the human tragedy that is so often glibly called "sin."

Secondly, we linger here because the story of Adam and Eve is not to be read as ancient history. The way in which the narrative is constructed bears the hallmarks of a master Hebrew storyteller, whose concern is not to present "history" as we understand the term today. Modern scholarly historical research is rightly concerned with supplying sufficient evidence to construct an authentic, historically accurate account of an event that took place in space and time. Genesis 1–3 does not afford us with that kind of literature. These narratives contain what we would today recognize as "mythical" elements—God "walking," dangerous forbidden trees, and a talking snake that does not, initially at least, crawl on its belly. These elements do not detract from the story; on the contrary, they enhance the intention of the storyteller. The Hebrew culture was not as concerned with "origins" as we are in our culture. The modern mind longs to know the answer to questions such as, "where did God come from?" or "what is the origin of evil?" To the ancient mind such questions were unanswerable and thus not worth asking. Rather, instead of asking questions dealing with origins, they were far more interested in causes. Why is this world so beautifully ordered? Why do human beings tend towards selfishness and greed at times and at other times show great creativity and joy? These are causal questions and ones that are addressed by the Genesis creation account.

The story of Adam and Eve thus needs to be approached with some degree of caution. A *literal* reading immediately leads towards ethical dilemmas. If the Lord God said to Adam and Eve, "Do not eat from the tree of the knowledge of good and evil or you will surely die," then the first transgression should have led to a swift fulfillment of that warning. Yet Adam and Eve did not die but were instead banished from the garden. Are we to conclude then that this was an empty threat from God? If so how can one take seriously any subsequent pronouncements from God? Is the word that comes from the mouth of the Lord to be trusted? Such questions suggest that an alternative reading needs to be sought. This is what Moberly argues for in his book *The Theology of the Book of Genesis*:

> The text provokes a reader into the kind of process that has been well articulated by Paul Ricoeur. An initial "first naiveté," when moral and religious teaching is taken straightforwardly and at face value, rightly gives way to a "critical distanciation," when it is realized that life and sacred texts are more complex and problematic than initially seemed to be the case . . . it is possible to move beyond it to a "second naiveté," where one learns to re-appropriate the moral and religious teaching in a deeper and more nuanced way.[9]

I suggest, therefore, that these foundational texts in the book of Genesis are to be read not merely as ancient stories with a high curiosity value, but rather as they were intended to be appropriated, namely "as a call to ground one's faith in the God of creation."[10] As such they cease to be detached from our world by a gaping distance of several thousand years, but they become our story too. The hugely influential Swiss theologian Karl Barth, writing in the middle of the twentieth century, made this comment about the story of Adam: "World history is Adamic history, the history of Adam. It began in and with this history, and—this is the Word and judgment of God on it, this is the explanation of its staggering monotony, this is the reason why there can never be any progress—it continually corresponds to this history. It is continually like it. With innumerable variations it constantly repeats it. It constantly re-enacts the little scene in the garden of Eden."[11] It is, in reality, a profoundly contemporary passage with

9. Moberly, *The Theology of the Book of Genesis*, 87.

10. Brueggemann, *Genesis*, 25.

11. Barth, *Church Dogmatics* IV/1, 508.

huge resonances with our world today. The name Adam (ʾ*ādām*) means "human being"—taken from the red soil (ʾ*ădāmâ*) of the earth, while the name Eve (*ḥawwâ*) means "life-giver." The ancient Hebrew storyteller is clearly crafting a tale about *all* of us, cleverly using first names that encompass the totality of the human race. This is a story that describes the condition in which humankind finds itself. *We are all Adam*, finding our origin in the dust of the earth itself; *we all are Eve*, alive with the very breath of God within us. The name Adam becomes therefore a representative name for the whole of humanity, which means that the story of "the fall" in Gen 3 is in reality the story of our daily choice to listen to the serpent rather than our creator. The story is a searing indictment of the way in which people in all places and times prefer to live independently of the God who created them and who loves them with a passion.

Yet the story is not only descriptive of human behavior and action in general; it is more searching than that. It is an account that is picked up by the Apostle Paul many centuries later and is included in the argumentation of his letters, particularly to the Romans and Corinthians. The force of his argument is profound. "For since death came through a man, the resurrection of the dead comes also through a man. For as in Adam all die, so in Christ all will be made alive" (1 Cor 15:22). Paul recounts the story of Adam and Eve in order to draw a parallel between the work of Christ and the consequences of the sin of Adam. His handling of the story indicates that he heard it as more than simply a descriptive account of who we are. Adam becomes a symbolic figure representing the entirety of the human race throughout all generations. It is in this sense that we are in Adam. Our identity as individuals is far more than a private, personal construction for we are intimately, unavoidably connected to the sum total of human community. Our ancestry is part of who we are and that ancestry is tainted, distorted, and dislocated. We may be born in innocence but we are not born into an innocent world. There is a pre-existent pathology that affects all of us passively, simply by virtue of being alive. We are not held responsible for that inherited distortion, for that would deny the very essence of human freedom and responsibility; but we are responsible for the choices we make that add further layers of distortion for succeeding generations. There is therefore an original sin that infects all of us. There is not and cannot be an original guilt, for to ascribe an original guilt to all of humanity is to render them culpable for an action for which they are not responsible. This is how McFadyen has articulated this notion of original sin: "The social processes through which we are called into full person-hood, the very processes through which we receive the conditions for au-tonomous and therefore responsible action, are pathologically distorted. They are alienated and alienating from God . . . We stand already, prior to any action on our part, in a pathological relationship to God—in sin."[12]

So the story of "the fall" and its consequences possesses a descriptive aspect—a description that depicts our very being, our ontology, as people who habitually choose to face away from their Creator. But it is also an account of our participation in the wider community of mankind, past and present—a community that is deeply flawed, and one that, tragically, transmits a distortion to each succeeding generation. It is a story that displays both the passive and the active aspects of sin.

Beginning with the creation narrative we have exposed the DNA of the human predicament that the Bible labels sin. This exposure, however, is merely a beginning, and it serves only to nudge us forward to explore how sin issues forth as the phenomenon of shame in a range of possible directions. Here we must gather together the fragments of evidence that the creation story has offered us.

The Phenomenon of Shame

The first avenue we will explore is concerned with *the corporate nature of shame*. Prior to their expulsion from the garden, Adam and Eve knew what it meant to belong and they belonged in a twofold sense. They belonged "geographically" in that they were placed, according to the narrative, in a location, a habitat, a space created for them in which they could flourish. I use the word "geographically" with some degree of caution as the mythi-cal elements of the story have already been noted. Yet the storyteller takes care to give us geographical details of the location of the garden, and the resultant expulsion from this home constituted a severe loss. The shame that followed from their tragic choice led to their dislocation from place, in fact it led directly to *exile*. We will need to trace how the theme of shame as exclusion and exile becomes a repeated refrain as the biblical narra-tives unfold. The exile of Adam and Eve foreshadowed the sense of exile experienced by the Jews in Egypt before their deliverance. Responding

12. McFadyen, *Bound to Sin*, 36–37.

to the catastrophe of shameful exile in Babylon becomes a challenge of acute proportions for the later generation of prophets and theologians. Jesus himself repeatedly sought out individuals in his ministry, as we shall see in due course, who suffered the ignominy of personal exile and exclusion from their own towns and cities. The connection between shame and belonging will be our first foray of investigation.

In second place we need to examine how shame and guilt are joined together. Adam and Eve's turning away from the face of God to listen to the tempting whisper of another caused them to make a desperate choice. It was a choice that signaled their dissatisfaction with the dependency of their lives on the God who had gifted them so abundantly. The result of their fateful choice was the experience of guilt, which was accompanied inevitably by shame. There is a connection therefore between guilt and shame but it is not an easy one to define. There are no clear linear paths from one to the other, and there are many times when people experience true shame without having experienced a prior guilt. There are undoubtedly many occasions too when shame does not arise from within but is placed on a person or a community from without. How guilt and shame speak to one another will be another line of enquiry we will need to follow.

Thirdly, there are psychological dimensions to shame that the creation story alludes to and one of those is the desire to hide or conceal. Adam and Eve exchanged their beautiful, open naïveté for suspicious hiding. No longer was there the freedom to be themselves before each other. We are given a picture of humanity that is at odds with itself, unable simply to *be*, afraid of being known, wanting to conceal, to run, to cover up. Depicted in these terms, the creation story has a sadly familiar and contemporary ring to it. Yet hiding was not the only psychological distortion that the story portrays. Once their misdemeanor is exposed, the instinctive response of Adam is to blame, to point the finger, to refuse to accept responsibility for his own actions. Blame had never been part of the original creation; it was not necessary, it was too aggressive, too violent a feature to have any place in the garden. Yet after their joint turning away from God, blame appears, ugly and destructive as always. Our third strand of questioning will need to explore these psychological dimensions of shame.

Fourthly, the story of the pair hiding from each other also includes their hiding from God. God comes looking for them, in much the same way as Christ himself would later declare that he came to seek and to save the lost. God's searching eyes find them crouching, cringing, wanting not to be found. Theirs is a spiritual crisis as well as a psychological one. What began as a spiritual relationship of beauty now becomes tarnished, characterized by avoidance and the averted gaze. They dare not look God in the eye any longer. How, then, can one depict the spirituality of shame? What are its manifestations? The creation story includes an intriguing, tiny detail, which is often overlooked. Adam and Eve are expelled from the garden and both have now to face the consequences of their choice. Yet in the midst of this devastation God does not abandon them to deal with their expulsion entirely alone. He provides them with leather coats to wear to keep them warm; in fact, he makes them himself. In order for God to be able to do this he will have to slaughter an animal whose coat is then offered to the couple for their protection. This small detail hints at the whole notion of sacrifice for the sake of another, and speaks of the grace and compassion of God in the midst of his searing judgment. The story of the fur coats made by God does not tell us much more than that, but simply introduces to us the idea that judgment, grace, mercy, and sacrifice go hand in hand and have much to say about the question of dealing with shame.

Lastly, our investigation will explore how the shame that the original couple experienced is connected to the body. The mention of nakedness and the subsequent desire to cover that nakedness suggests that the distorting effect of sin has a deep connection with the very physicality of our being. Does the Bible have anything to say about the role and significance of our flesh and blood both in the experience of shame and its redemption and healing? Is there a connection therefore between the original nakedness in the garden and the utter redemptive nakedness of Christ's exposed body on the cross?

This list offers a depiction of the phenomena of shame and provides us with investigative leads, all of which offer us a different shade of meaning as we explore the question of shame—belonging, guilt, psychology, spirituality, grace, and our own physicality. At a later stage, having explored what each of these concepts means in relation to shame, we will need to build bridges to the work of Christ, his life as well as his death and resurrection. The writer of the Letter to the Hebrews gives us a clue that such a bridge is indeed possible when he depicts the crucifixion of Christ as having a profound connection with shame, for it was there that Christ "despised" the shame of the cross thus making it a place of healing (Heb 12:2). The apostle Paul too found that the good news of Jesus Christ—the gospel—was something about which he felt no shame at all (Rom 1:16). The New Testament tells us that the coming of Christ into the world needs to be understood as speaking to the pressing, urgent, desperate need to bring healing to a shamed world. How that healing, that salvation, that finding of honor can be brought into effect will form the substance of the later chapters of this book, yet even at this early stage of our exploration there are hints that it will be profoundly connected with the question of the face of God. The turning away from God in guilt and shame was a turning away from his *pānîm*, his face. The restoration of Cain, if it had ever happened, would have resulted in the lifting up of his face. Thus "face" as a theological category needs to be explored in the light of the problem that needs to be addressed. If the problem of humanity's sin is located primarily as one of guilt, then immediately we are using a *legal* term that will necessitate a *legal* solution. This is not to deny the validity of legal metaphors, for, as we shall see, the apostle Paul uses a variety of metaphors—military, medical, social, cultic, and financial, in addition to legal—in his attempts to draw out the meaning of Christ's atoning work. If sin is framed in terms of shame, however, then a legal solution to something as deep and existential as shame will be inappropriate. Shame is such an intensely personal experience, having both corporate and private dimensions, that an intensely personal remedy needs to be applied. The notion of the face of God (and, later, the face of Christ) offers us precisely this intimate address to the predicament that humanity finds itself in.

3

Belonging

BELONGING IS SUCH A vital, essential aspect of human existence that it seems almost facile to state it. We live in communities of families, villages, towns, cities, and nations all of which hold us in a place where we are able to function. These communities offer us a habitat for living and a foothold in a web of interconnected, complex relationships, without which human beings find it almost impossible to exist. It is no accident that the most severe form of punishment that most Western societies can administer is to impose solitary confinement on its most difficult, dangerous, and violent criminals. To be without any human contact at all is to be excluded from any possible form of belonging. It should come as no surprise that our need to belong has strong theological roots. If we are made in the image of God, we bear the imprint of the creator within the very heart of who we are. One aspect of that image is that God is intrinsically *relational*—Father, Son, and Holy Spirit; a community of persons; a being-in-communion. That is who God *is*, and it is according to this pattern that we as humans are constituted. We only truly find out who we are in the presence of another who stands before us. The touching story of Mary and Elizabeth in Luke's Gospel illustrates this perfectly. Elizabeth's tale begins with the opening verses of Luke's Gospel. After her husband's dramatic experience while on duty in the temple, he returns home, silent, and soon afterwards Elizabeth notices that, to her amazement and delight, she is finally pregnant. Her response to this discovery is recorded by Luke: "In these days he has shown his favor and taken away my disgrace among the people" (Luke 1:25).

Her immediate interpretation of the news of impending motherhood is that her *disgrace*—or shame—will be taken away. The word translated here as "disgrace," *oneidos*, is a strong noun and is used again, as we shall see in due course, by Paul in some of his letters. It carries the sense of "an object of reproach," "a person who is reviled," whose name, character, and reputation are called into question. Such was the strength of feeling attached to childlessness, a condition that placed the barren woman at a distance from full inclusion in the community. It was clearly a burden that Elizabeth had borne her entire adult life and now, in her later years, this crushing sense of shame was being lifted. Her utterance reveals much about the corporate nature of shame and how central it was to life among ancient Jewish communities. Elizabeth's joy is compounded once she meets her cousin Mary. The young Mary has received the news from the angel that she is to bear the Christ child. She is very young to carry such an enormous responsibility, and so she seeks out the support and friendship of her cousin Elizabeth, who, like her, is carrying a child.

> When Elizabeth heard Mary's greeting, the baby leaped in her womb, and Elizabeth was filled with the Holy Spirit. In a loud voice she exclaimed: "Blessed are you among women, and blessed is the child you will bear! But why am I so favored, that the mother of my Lord should come to me? As soon as the sound of your greeting reached my ears, the baby in my womb leaped for joy. Blessed is she who has believed that what the Lord has said to her will be accomplished!" And Mary said: "My soul glorifies the Lord and my spirit rejoices in God my Savior." (Luke 1:41–47)

When the two women meet, the encounter elicits a burst of praise from Elizabeth, which in turn appears to unlock from within Mary the extraordinary Magnificat. The way in which Luke has constructed the story suggests that the two women needed one another in order to truly know themselves. As they stood facing each other in warm embrace, perhaps for the first time they knew who they were within the greater narrative of God's redemption. Although this story depicts the account of two individuals meeting each other, in reality we need more than that. We need to be included in a wider community with its own rituals and customs: a place of safety in which human life can flourish. The community is the

God-given habitat in which human beings were always intended to live. To belong to society and to be fully accepted is to find honor; by contrast to be excluded from community is to endure ignominy and shame of the most acute kind. If we search the Old Testament, for example, for a thoroughgoing theological interpretation of what it means to be an individual human being, apart from our interconnections with others, there is virtually no evidence of such a concept at all. It appears that there is no interest in developing a theological anthropology of the individual—it is "not even on the horizon of Old Testament witness," as the theologian Walter Brueggemann has put it.[1] The reason for this striking absence is that humanness was perceived to be a function of belonging to a community, both to the covenantal community of Israel and to the community of God, who called and shaped that odd collection of tribes into a nation in the first place. To be human in the fullest, most biblical sense is to belong, to be held, nurtured, and protected by the larger web of relationships within which one's own life can flourish. This sense of belonging is intrinsically inter-dependent and never competitive. To belong is to acknowledge one's need both to give and to receive, to be both strong and weak, to make oneself accountable and vulnerable to others. It is hard to overstate the critical importance of this profoundly corporate dimension to our humanity. It is not surprising, therefore, to find that when that place of belonging is put in jeopardy the specter of shame raises its head. To be excluded from community is not a mere inconvenience; it strikes at our core identity, it questions our right to exist, it threatens our perception of ourselves and our communion with God.

Belonging to the Nation of Israel

The culture into which Jesus was born was tainted with the distorting effects of the competition to determine who truly belonged to the community of Israel and who had forfeited their right to do so. The struggle for dominance was played out by four major sectarian groups, each exhibiting its own version of exclusion. The Zealot movement was one of these. They took as their inspiration the actions of Phineas, depicted in Num 25, who was consumed with zeal for the Lord, which manifested itself in violence. His murderous behavior towards an Israelite who had dared to

1. Brueggemann, *Theology of the Old Testament*, 450.

copulate with a Moabitess—thereby exposing Israel to the danger of being drawn towards the idolatry of Moab—was seen as a means of averting the wrath of Yahweh. The role model taken by these first-century Zealots legitimized their own violence against the occupying Roman forces and against Jews perceived as siding with Rome. The oppressive system of Roman taxation fueled their anger, for the majority of the impoverished members of society remained locked into an unending cycle of debt repayments often resulting in enslavement. The second major group was the Pharisees, who passionately believed that the coming of the kingdom of God on earth would only be achieved through a strict adherence to their own oral tradition of religious laws. Their strenuous enforcement of this mindset demanded a policing role within society, in which they publicly denounced those who did not conform. Robert Jewett describes the way in which the Pharisees operated: "Religious performances of fasting, almsgiving, and praying were prominent features of the Pharisee program to demonstrate the superior honor of their sect and to reinforce the conformity that would allegedly lead to the establishment of Israel as the capitol of the world instead of Rome. Religion was being used here in the reinforcement of a system of social superiority."[2]

The third group was the Essenes, who advocated a separatist withdrawal from what they perceived to be a corrupt society. Only by observing their own cultic traditions, which included celibacy, daily purification rituals, and the communal ownership of property, would the messianic age be ushered in. The final group was the Sadducees, who placed great emphasis on temple worship, rejected any notion of resurrection, and did not believe that there were rewards or punishments after death. In their role as guardians of the temple they were willing to cooperate with the Roman authorities, much to the chagrin of the Zealots and the Essenes.

While each of these different groups had very disparate sets of beliefs, they shared the same toxic values. Theirs was a competitive world in which one must jostle for a place of honor within both the coming kingdom and within contemporary society. Those who did not share their values, who polluted their world, thereby delaying or hindering their advancement of those goals, could be shunned, excluded, and vilified. It was a poisonous system of exclusion and shaming and one to which allusion is often made throughout the Gospels. Take, for example, the admonition

2. Jewett, "Got Good Religion?," 187–208.

given by Jesus in his Sermon on the Mount: "Beware of practicing your piety before men in order to be seen by them" (Matt 6:1). To what is Jesus referring? He is bringing to the attention of his hearers the public actions of the religious elite of his day. They would recite eloquent prayers in the public arena in their quest to climb the ladder of increasing honor. As Ben Witherington puts it, "in an honor and shame culture one is always trying to improve one's rating."[3] This was a competition that the poor could never win. Without access to the formal means of education, most could not read and write, so that to utter a prayer in public would simply be to invite further ridicule. The mere act of praying ostentatiously served only to emphasize how distant the poor were from full inclusion in society. The antidote to this kind of activity is offered immediately as Jesus' sermon proceeds. He says, "Go into your room, close the door, and pray to your Father who is unseen." The Greek word translated here as "room" is *tameion*, a word used to describe a small storehouse for grain and tools. It was certainly never considered to be a place of intimate communion with God. In fact the very suggestion is filled with a kind of mischievous humor, intended to elicit the response of the raised eyebrow in amazement. It is an example of Jesus debunking the precious, pious super-spirituality of his day, which, in its effects, was profoundly oppressive. This saying of Jesus cuts at the root of the competition for honor in the society of which he was a part. For the "hypocrites" who practiced their piety in full view, the reward was a reputation for being pious and therefore, by implication, for being honorable people. Those who followed the teachings of Jesus, however, withdrew from such practices, thereby depriving themselves of any chance of achieving an honorable status.

What lay behind the culture of competing for honor and its counterpart, the distribution of shame, was a theology that yearned for the manifestation, at some indeterminate point in the future, of the kingdom of God, which would finally vanquish Israel's enemies and place God's chosen land, people, and city in their rightful place of prominence. However, if the kingdom of God had already arrived, as Jesus repeatedly proclaimed that it had,[4] then all such competitive behavior for inclusion in God's society became totally superfluous. If all were welcome in the

---

3. Witherington, *Matthew*, 240.

4. E.g., Matt 4:17: "From that time on Jesus began to preach, 'Repent, for the kingdom of heaven has come near.'"

kingdom then eloquent public prayer was unnecessary. If the kingdom of God was present *now*, then pious actions done with an eye to accruing more honor were utterly unnecessary. From now on they could be done in secret, with the left hand not even knowing what the right hand was doing. Once the kingdom of God is seen as a *gift* rather than a reward, then there is no longer a place for competitive behavior. Such competition only produces winners as well as losers, the included as well as the excluded, the ones who have acquired a false kind of honor and those who have been shamed.

Appreciating the pervasive influence of the honor and shame dynamic sheds light on many of the New Testament narratives. We may take, for example, the parable of the Friend at Midnight in Luke 11:5–8.

> Then he said to them, "Suppose one of you has a friend, and he goes to him at midnight and says, 'Friend, lend me three loaves of bread, because a friend of mine on a journey has come to me, and I have nothing to set before him.' Then the one inside answers, 'Don't bother me. The door is already locked, and my children are with me in bed. I can't get up and give you anything.' I tell you, though he will not get up and give him the bread because he is his friend, yet because of the man's boldness he will get up and give him as much as he needs."

How are we to interpret this parable? To the modern reader it seems as if the owner of the house only decides to open the door of his home after he is worn down by the persistence of the friend who knocks on his door at midnight. The interpretative emphasis is placed on the action of the friend who refuses to give up, with the obvious corollary that if we keep pestering the doors of heaven, God will eventually answer our prayers because he is simply worn out by our persistence. The view of God that this interpretation presents is an unfortunate one. God appears reluctant to hear the cries of the desperate and will only deign to rouse himself if he is sufficiently provoked by our persistence. This cannot be the implicit interpretation of this parable, for it offers a disincentive to approach God in trusting faith. Kenneth Bailey offers an entirely different configuration of this parable based on his experience of having lived in the Middle East for most of his life and having studied the culture of that part of the world. The import of this parable turns around a key question which Bailey paraphrases thus: "Can you imagine having a guest and going to a neighbor to borrow bread and the neighbor offers ridiculous excuses about a locked door and sleeping children?" To the Middle Eastern mind the obvious response would be "No, I couldn't imagine such a thing!"[5] The reason for this is that the parable hinges around the question of a sense of honor and the blamelessness of the man who is asleep. Bailey points out that the guest who arrives from being on a journey would have been considered to be the guest of the whole community not just the individual. Thus the community was responsible for his welfare and had an obligation to offer him hospitality. The significance of the passage lies in the interpretation of the Greek word *anaideia*, translated in the NIV as "boldness." The translators have made the decision that the positive quality of boldness or persistence is to be applied to the friend who arrives at midnight and continues knocking at the door. Bailey suggests that this makes little sense linguistically, theologically, or culturally. The word *anaideia* refers not to the visitor but to *the owner* of the house, and it does not mean boldness in this context. It is far better, claims Bailey, to translate the word as "the avoidance of shame." Once this is clear the parable takes on a new meaning. It is because the sleeping man wants to avoid shaming the entire village community by failing to provide sustenance for the traveler, that he will—of course—get up and provide bread. The parable thus deals with both the nature of God as well as the injunction to persist in prayer. One may draw encouragement to prayer precisely because God wishes to honor the one praying and indeed the entire praying community—*that* gives the parable its potency. Bailey summarizes the impact of the story thus: "The parable said to the original listener. 'When you go to this kind of a neighbor everything is against you. It is night. He is asleep in bed. The door is locked. His children are asleep. He does not like you and yet you will receive even more than you ask. This is because your neighbor is a man of integrity and he will not violate that quality. The God to whom you pray also has integrity and he will not violate you either.'"[6]

The story of the birth of Jesus contains some significant illustrations concerning the way in which a concern to avoid public shame or disgrace is a powerful driving force. Matthew's Gospel records the reaction of Mary's betrothed husband Joseph to the news that she is pregnant. In his book *Honor, Patronage, Kinship and Purity*, David deSilva has highlighted

5. Bailey, *Poet and Peasant*, 119.

6. Ibid., 133.

the way in which the duties of kinship required that members of the family who were found to be in a place of shame, be shielded from public exposure and disgrace.[7] Given this cultural insight one can immediately understand Joseph's response. "Because Joseph her husband was a righteous man and did not want to expose her to public disgrace, he had in mind to divorce her quietly" (Matt 1:19). Just as Elizabeth's disgrace of childlessness had been taken away by the birth of John, as we have already observed, so Mary is now in danger of being publicly disgraced. It was Joseph's duty as a member of her kinship group to protect her from such a fate. A public act of shaming would place Mary at risk of having no valid place within society. Yet, as Joseph was later to realize, the entire life of Mary's son was to be dominated by issues of disgrace and shame. Luke's account of the birth narrative further illustrates this connection between shame and belonging. Jesus is born in a simple peasant home and placed in a manger. This would have been common practice in the homes of such people in those days, but the surprise in the story comes with the angelic announcement to the shepherds in Luke 2:8ff. At the time, shepherds were poor and in Rabbinic tradition were labeled as "unclean." They were at the very bottom of the social ladder and lived nomadic, solitary lives. To be considered in such a lowly position was to be without honor, in a place of shame. Yet it is *these* people who are the first to be told the news of the birth of the Messiah. Understandably they were terrified. How could they—despised shepherds—visit a home where the long-awaited Messiah was laid? To assuage their terror the angel offers them a sign—it is the sign of the manger. Immediately they would have known that this newborn king was not lying in the home of a wealthy landowner who might turn them away with a wave of his hand. No, the manger was a sign that Jesus was born in the home of simple poor peasants, exactly the same as their own. This was wonderful news, news that meant that they would be welcomed by the owners of the home and that they would be able to pay their respects to the young family. It was abundantly evident now that God had "lifted up the humble" (Luke 1:52). Here, then, right at the beginning of the narrative of Jesus, we see the shamed being honored and included as key players in an unfolding drama.

The public ministry of Jesus further develops the inclusion of the shamed members of society. All four Gospel writers record the anger that

7. deSilva, *Honor, Patronage, Kinship and Purity*, 171.

Jesus displays when clearing out the temple, and while John places the event at the beginning of Jesus' ministry, the Synoptic writers choose to insert this story towards the end of their narratives. Its placement here is significant, for these actions of Jesus are depicted as the last public engagement prior to his death. Within a week of this cleansing, Jesus is dead. It is as if Jesus chooses to bring matters to a head, to ignite the final chapter of his mission and to complete, through a symbolic act, the task that he was given to do. The significance of the temple cleansing lies not so much in the activity of money changing. This was a standard practice and was intended to be a service to pilgrims who required temple coinage to fulfill the requirements of liturgical worship. Rather, Jesus' anger was kindled by the *location* of the business activity. This trade took place within the outer courts of the temple precincts, including the court of the Gentiles. This court was the only place where those outside of the Hebrew covenant could taste something of the grace of God, and it was the occupancy of this precise space that hindered these outsiders from doing so. Their invitation to the place of inclusion was rendered impossible by the greed of those rogue traders. No wonder Jesus got so angry. Here the excluded could have found a home, and yet here their exclusion is perpetuated. By throwing these traders out of the court of the Gentiles he was declaring the scope of his mission. It was to include those who for so long had been excluded, to say to those who felt the burden of shame that they too could approach the place of grace without fear or hindrance. In that one action Jesus encapsulated the essence of his redeeming search and its effect was explosive. At last the authorities could see clearly the extent of the subversive nature of the good news, the arrival of which Jesus had announced so frequently. If this kind of inclusive gospel was allowed to take root then the entire system of honor and shame that had become so firmly established over centuries would be turned upside down. With such a Messiah, those who were unclean, unworthy, and therefore profoundly unwelcome, would be given equal footing with everyone else. Unthinkable! This man must be silenced! Time and again Jesus purposely sought out those on the margins of society: the leper, the Samaritan, the prostitute, the tax collector. It is clear that the intention of the Gospel writers is to allow their stories to unfold in our imagination so that a picture of Jesus emerges as one who reverses these exclusions. He goes to the places where the shamed are found and he reconciles them through conversation or healing touch.

Shame and Kinship

A central feature of the communal nature of shame and honor in the Bible is the question of the perpetuation of the family name. In Hebrew culture it was vitally necessary to preserve the family name so that the memory of that family would not be lost. The collective memory of the name ensured continuity not only with the contemporary community, but also with communities long since gone. Belonging to past and present communities gave some degree of assurance that belonging in the future may continue. The story of God's redemption recorded in the Bible emerged from a culture in which genealogy was critically important. There are a number of such lists of family histories (e.g., Gen 10; 1 Chr 1–9; Matt 1) and their significance cannot be overstated. By recording a person's lineage one can find a place for that person within communities over time and in space. A genealogy is a coded message about the claim that a person has to status, rank, or power. Someone whose function was to serve as a priest would need to demonstrate his genealogical credentials, which provided evidence that he was a "son of Aaron." Likewise when Jesus dramatically encounters the despised tax collector Zaccheus, he declares at the end of their conversation that this man, astonishingly, can now be counted as a "son of Abraham." The function of kinship within the Bible cannot be overstated, for it was by means of kinship that one's honor was protected.

A good example of the critical significance of this is illustrated by the case of Hannah. Her distress is recorded in all its anguish in 1 Sam 1, which tells the story of one woman who feared that her lack of a male heir would in turn lead to the loss of her place in the continuance of the family name.

> This went on year after year. Whenever Hannah went up to the house of the LORD, her rival provoked her till she wept and would not eat. Elkanah her husband would say to her, "Hannah, why are you weeping? Why don't you eat? Why are you downhearted? Don't I mean more to you than ten sons?" Once, when they had finished eating and drinking in Shiloh, Hannah stood up. Now Eli the priest was sitting on a chair by the doorpost of the LORD's temple. In bitterness of soul Hannah wept much and prayed to the LORD. And she made a vow, saying, "O LORD Almighty, if you will only look upon your servant's misery and remember me, and not forget your servant but give her a son, then I will give him to

> the LORD for all the days of his life, and no razor will ever be used on his head." (1 Sam 1:7–11)

Hannah's inability to bear a son made her the object of the scorn and derision of Peninnah, the other wife of Elkanah, who heaped humiliation upon her, year after year. Hannah feels this shame acutely and even the loving encouragements of her husband cannot soothe her pain. She cries out to the Lord from the depths that the Lord would "remember her," a phrase which denotes that the face of God would be turned fully in her direction. The only adequate way for Hannah to be sure of this divine remembering would be if she could produce a son. Her husband, Elkanah, is introduced to us at the outset of the book, via means of his genealogy. The rhetorical purpose of this inclusion is to define who he is in relation to his ancestry. He has two wives through whom his family name could be perpetuated, and although his second wife, Peninnah, has produced sons, the emphasis of the story lies with the first wife, Hannah, and the problem of her barrenness. Walter Brueggemann comments on Hannah's tortured dilemma in this way. "From his fathers, Elkanah has a proud past. With his wife [Hannah], however, he has no future. The story invites us with Israel to reflect on this question, How is a new future possible amid barrenness that renders us bitter, hopeless, and fruitless?"[8] It is the anticipated threat of a future in which Hannah plays no part that is the source of her shame. The disgrace that Hannah experienced was due to the fear that, without a son, she herself could not participate in a future within the family line of her husband.

There are a number of Old Testament texts that further illustrate this essentially corporate nature of shame. The story in Deut 25:5–10 describes a situation where a man dies and leaves a widow without an heir.

> If brothers are living together and one of them dies without a son, his widow must not marry outside the family. Her husband's brother shall take her and marry her and fulfill the duty of a broth-er-in-law to her. The first son she bears shall carry on the name of the dead brother so that his name will not be blotted out from Israel. However, if a man does not want to marry his brother's wife, she shall go to the elders at the town gate and say, "My husband's brother refuses to carry on his brother's name in Israel. He will not fulfill the duty of a brother-in-law to me." Then the elders of his

8. Brueggemann, *First and Second Samuel*, 12.

town shall summon him and talk to him. If he persists in saying, "I do not want to marry her," his brother's widow shall go up to him in the presence of the elders, take off one of his sandals, spit in his face and say, "This is what is done to the man who will not build up his brother's family line." That man's line shall be known in Israel as "The Family of the Unsandaled."

This story illustrates the anxiety that arises in the event of the death of a man who does not yet have a son. His widow will be left in a situation in which she is unable to have a child with the result that she will have no heir to perpetuate the family name. If the family name does not continue then the shame of being forgotten becomes a real possibility. How can the threat of shame be averted? The Deuteronomic provisions offer a solution. It is the duty of the dead man's brother to marry the widow in order that she might conceive a son who could then carry on the family name. If the surviving brother refuses to do this, the widow has the right to go to the elders of the city to ask them to intervene on her behalf. If the brother persists in refusing to marry her, she "shall go up to him in the presence of the elders, take off one of his sandals, spit in his face and say, 'This is what is done to the man who will not build up his brother's family line.' That man's line shall be known in Israel as 'The Family of the Unsandaled.'" The significance of the spitting and sandal removing is important. The surviving brother had brought shame on the widow and therefore on his own brother by refusing to perform his expected duty. The consequence was that he, in turn, would be shamed by the community. In the act of spitting, a bodily substance leaves the body, which in Hebrew thought was understood to be a bounded system, symbolic of the whole community. Once fluids leave the body they become unclean. The removing of the sandal may have symbolized the loss of property to the brother-in-law if the widow subsequently married outside the family, or it may have had a more sexual connotation, as in Ruth 3:1–7.[9] The impact of

---

9. "One day Naomi, her mother-in-law, said to her, 'My daughter, should I not try to find a home for you, where you will be well provided for? Is not Boaz, with whose servant girls you have been, a kinsman of ours? Tonight he will be winnowing barley on the threshing-floor. Wash and perfume yourself, and put on your best clothes. Then go down to the threshing-floor, but don't let him know you are there until he has finished eating and drinking. When he lies down, note the place where he is lying. Then go and uncover his feet and lie down. He will tell you what to do.' 'I will do whatever you say,' Ruth answered. So she went down to the threshing-floor and did everything her mother-in-law told her to do. When Boaz had finished eating and drinking and was in good

this dual action was very serious. The brother would have had to live with a shamed reputation for the rest of his life with the likelihood of exclusion from the community. The shaming sanction could have threatened his very survival. Yet in the same chapter of Deuteronomy there is a concern that shaming should not be excessive. In verses 1–3 there are instructions concerning the number of times a man may be flogged after having been found guilty by a court. He must not receive more than forty lashes or he would be degraded (shamed) in the eyes of the community.

Another example may be cited from Deut 22:28–29: "If a man happens to meet a virgin who is not pledged to be married and rapes her and they are discovered, he shall pay the girl's father fifty shekels of silver. He must marry the girl, for he has violated her. He can never divorce her as long as he lives." This rather extraordinary law sounds repugnant to modern ears. Why should a woman who has been violated be obliged to marry the man who has committed this crime? The answer lies in the cultural emphasis on honor and shame and in the pressing need to ensure survival. It would have been commonplace in those days for a woman who had been raped to be regarded as impure and shamed, even though she was the innocent victim of an abusive act. Such a woman would have found it impossible to marry and would therefore have struggled to survive without a man to support her. Her whole future existence would have been placed in jeopardy by this one event, and it is precisely because she was the innocent victim that she must be protected and looked after for the remainder of her life. The man who has violated her must take on this responsibility for it is he who has brought shame upon her and so it must be he who makes amends. The injunction that he is to marry her was made for her own future security and for her restoration into the wider community.

Taken together these biblical narratives progressively build up a view of the landscape of the corporate nature of shame. It is found wherever there is a failure or inability to live up to societal ideals, identifications, and roles, which dictate expectations of what a person should be able to do, know, or feel. Shame is therefore experienced in situations of incongruity, where expectations are reversed or not met or where there is inappropriateness of some kind. There is a powerful dynamic in opera-

---

spirits, he went over to lie down at the far end of the grain pile. Ruth approached quietly, uncovered his feet, and lay down."

tion here, articulated in the fear of expulsion, separation, abandonment, or insignificance. Indeed the fear of insignificance is perhaps the most central human fear of all. Shame can be understood, therefore, as arising from the external pressure of a group, where the use of shame as a social sanction is particularly effective. Shame is closely related to the reception of approval such that the experience of being shamed, or the withdrawal of approval, strikes at the core of who a person is. Shame and anxiety thus become inseparable companions. The fear of being shamed leads to a state of anxious anticipation, which in turn leads to a whole range of coping mechanisms being established.

What does it mean therefore to belong? The biblical texts that we have explored in this chapter have illustrated how belonging is far from being a peripheral issue in human experience. To belong is to dwell in a habitat in which one's life can flourish. It is to be held in a web of relationships that will support, encourage, guide, and accompany someone through life. To know that one can simply belong without preconditions, without the need to perform, is to be in a place of safety and liberty. This experience, however, is not merely a psychological necessity, nor is it only a mechanism by which societies construct meaning for themselves. We need to belong, because that is how we have been created—as creatures that are dependent and in need of community in order to be able to thrive. If God himself dwells within a community of persons—Father, Son, and Holy Spirit—it is inconceivable that we could do otherwise. To be in a place where the sense of belonging is questioned or placed in jeopardy is not merely an inconvenient irritation; it strikes at the very heart of what it means to be human. That is why shame and honor, exclusion and belonging are inextricably linked together.

4

Shame and Guilt

IT IS NOW TIME to look more closely at the relationship between shame and guilt. These two terms are relatives belonging to the same family, connected via history, sharing similar characteristics, yet are distinctively and qualitatively different. According to the Christian tradition, the distortion and violence of the world we now inhabit is caused by the entry of "sin." How can we give content to this little word that has become so emotionally laden with often oppressive controlling overtones? Is it simply a moral assessment of a particular action? How has this word and its derivatives come to be used as a weapon heaping abuse and further disgrace on those deemed to deserve its appellation? In embarking on this investigative journey we must be careful with the use of language. Often communication is hampered by the assumption that we instinctively know what certain forms of language mean. Language is slippery, supple, and capable of an "overflow of possibilities," to borrow a phrase from Paul Ricoeur. A particular sound—for example "tree"—possesses meaning because we are able to refer the sound of the word "tree" to the reality of trees that we see all around us. This is the way language works.

The language of the Bible is full of surprises in that it takes ordinary words that are entirely familiar and gives them an utterly different meaning such that the stability of our perception of the world is profoundly subverted. A good example of this is found in Christ's trial before Pilate. Pilate challenges Jesus with the question, "Are you a king?" As he asks this question, it is clear that Pilate is referring to his concept of king, namely an earthly ruler, with authority over his subjects, with power to wield the sword, who implicitly is a threat to the rule of Caesar in Rome. His usage of the word "king" in this simple question betrays his own understanding of the term. Jesus answers this question in the affirmative, "Yes I am," he says. But it is immediately obvious that whilst both parties in this conversation are using the same *word*—king—they are giving the word *utterly different meanings*. Jesus' usage of the term "king" means something like this: "the one who comes to serve, to give his life for the sake of others, to enter the dark and shameful places where the outcasts dwell." That is what Jesus alludes to in using the term "king," and that is the meaning that Pilate failed to perceive. Time and again the Bible confounds us with altered meanings that usher in new perspectives and open up alternative horizons. As we progress through this investigation, we will need to pause from time to time to check whether our understanding of the language of biblical narrative is correct.

We have already explored, through the Genesis narrative, how the unwelcome intruder of "sin" broke into the beautiful world that God had fashioned. In the history of Christian thought there is a considerable spectrum of opinion concerning how to understand the nature of this intrusion. The predominant term that has consumed the energies of theologians—at least in the Western theological tradition—has been "guilt," and this metaphor has defined, shaped, and molded subsequent theological reflections as a result. Within this interpretative framework the long shadow of Augustine can be detected. The predicament that we find ourselves in is placed within the Creation–Fall–Redemption paradigm that he so eloquently espoused, a paradigm in which the term "sin" is understood as disobedience to the divine command. The guilt that ensues needs to be forgiven in order for the sinner to be restored into a right relationship with the Creator. The only way in which forgiveness can occur is through the sacrificial atoning death of Christ, which diverts or propitiates the wrath of the Father by satisfying the demands of justice. This version of events begins, therefore, with the big problem of human guilt. When sin is defined principally as a transgression against an abstract law then the resultant legal status of the one who has committed the transgression is one of guilt. If this is how our status before God is depicted then the "solution" to our damaged status must turn around questions that deal with either the punishment or the remission of that guilt. It is an entirely logical chain of reasoning, yet one is left with the impression of a cosmos that is constructed around a cold, mathematical system of legal exchange. Within this theoretical construction we are immediately ushered via a legal metaphor into the heavenly courtroom, where ideas of judge and accused and questions of guilt and innocence, punishment or release have key places.

If the story of the redeeming work of Christ is told primarily in this way then we might expect the New Testament to be full of depictions and reflections on the pervasive evidence of guilt. Yet the Greek word for "guilty," *enochos*, only appears eight times altogether and in the King James Version at least it is normally translated as "danger," as can be seen for example in Matt 5:21: "Ye have heard that it was said by them of old time, Thou shalt not kill; and whosoever shall kill shall be in danger [*enochos*] of the judgment." This paucity of evidence is surprising given the overwhelming emphasis placed on guilt in countless sermons and theological studies. It is perhaps an unfortunate and unwelcome emphasis given that the heartbeat of the Bible, the engine room as it were, is *relationship* rather than law. This is not to say that legal metaphors have no place, it is simply to say that they should not be center stage. When Jesus taught his disciples to pray, he began with the language of the family—our Father—not the language of the judge's bench. It would be strange indeed for Jesus to issue an invitation to approach God without fear or dread as a Father only to discover that behind that welcoming embrace lies the cold logic of judicial mathematics. The language of shame, being inherently relational, suggests that an alternative paradigm for sin needs to be explored further. If we make this our starting point, then the life and ministry of Jesus may begin to look very different. Shame does not carry a legal meaning in the way that guilt appears to. It sounds far more personal, more existential, more corporate. Could it be that shame as a theological category has been tragically overlooked, especially when we attempt to build a bridge from shame to the entire mission of Christ? What does that mission look like when shame enters the picture? This is a question that will be addressed more fully in a later chapter.

We need, however, at this point to return to the question of the relationship between shame and guilt and to place that within the broader context of the term "sin." A quick tour of the history of Christian thought on this question illustrates the diverse ways in which the collective term "sin" has been interpreted. One of the earliest attempts at defining sin came from a heretical Christian group, the Manichees. They had asserted that sin has its root in the human body; the sheer physicality of our being is the root cause of our spiritual cancer. If our bodies are the cause of the problem, then the solution must surely lie in our escape from them, so that we can once more be pure spirit untainted by the evils of the flesh. In sharp contrast to this Manichean thinking, Augustine of Hippo, one of the earliest theologians who sought to construct a comprehensive theological structure for the Christian faith, reacted strongly against this kind of dualistic thinking. True, the body is often bedeviled by lust and fornication, claimed Augustine, but our physical world is surely a gift of the Creator, and that includes our human bodies too. Augustine therefore rejected the Manichean view and instead proposed that sin was fundamentally a relational issue. It concerned the way in which humanity chose to enter into and maintain a relationship with God, and when this relationship became broken or distorted then the cause could be named quite simply as pride. Augustine believed that our whole lives centered around our longings, our desires for intimacy, and for a true, deep connection with God. These longings are indicative of our need to be dependent people. We were never created to live isolated, independent lives, detached from others or from the God who made us. We were made for relationship and it is precisely because of this that we feel such an existential need within us for communion. When humankind suppresses or denies these God-given longings and chooses an independent existence, without any dependent relationships at all, then this is indicative of the proud characteristic of sin. In this way, Augustine constructed a framework that offered an interpretation of the distorted and tragic nature of our world.

Some one thousand years later another theologian entered the discussion on the nature of sin: Martin Luther. His struggles with the Scriptures in the context of a corrupt and oppressive mediaeval Roman Catholicism, led him to adopt a vivid metaphor regarding the nature of sin. It was, claimed Luther, nothing other than the inward curve of the human spirit upon itself. This inward turn, spiraling away from any other, resulted in an obsession with one's own self to the exclusion of God and, no doubt, to the exclusion of other significant human relationships. Luther offered an image of the self that was created for relationship yet that had chosen, perversely, to twist back on itself in a fatally damaging manner. Early in the twentieth century Karl Barth constructed an understanding of sin that took the person of Jesus Christ as a reference point, the ultimate criterion, of what it means to be truly human. Jesus lived before the face of his heavenly Father in perfect mutual harmony. The two were one, bound together in the love of the Holy Spirit, such that Jesus could declare that in his earthly ministry he walked in perfect unison with his Father; they were a team, cooperating in the work of seeking and saving the lost. This, then, is the pattern for our humanity. Just as Jesus lives in communion with the Father, so we as finite creatures find our true selves in communion with others and with God. This is what is known as the "I–You" encounter.[1] If I face another person in a healthy open relationship, then I will see the other before me as an equal—different, yet the same kind of creature. I, as an individual, need others to complement and complete who I am. There is simultaneously an *in*dependence from the "other"—I am uniquely me—*and* an *inter*dependence with the other, which is profoundly necessary for me to fully know who I am. This is the way we are made—with and for others, with and for God.

The entry of sin into the world has profoundly distorted this and Barth suggested that there are two false forms of human encounter. One of these forms happens when I, as an individual, lessen myself before another person and make myself nothing. Instead of a healthy "I–You"[2] relationship of mutuality, we end up with "o–You," and our own sense of self is lost. The disappearance of the sense and the value of oneself is a damaging, sinful distortion of who we are. If God makes each of us in his image as unique individuals then our value is assured and should never be dispensed with. The second and opposite distortion is when "I–You" becomes "I–It." This may occur when we choose to see the other facing

1. Barth wrote about I-thou mainly in CD III/2, 101, 108, 194, and 251. He was undoubtedly influenced by the Jewish philosopher Martin Buber.

2. Cf. Martin Buber's significant work *I-Thou* was published in 1923. What is perhaps less well known is that the idea of defining the nature of the self was pre-figured by Samuel Taylor Coleridge over one hundred years earlier. In his book *Opus Maximum* he writes, "but if the reader will place himself so far in the same state of Self-observation as the writer, he will discover that the consciousness expressed in the term 'thou' is only possible by an equation in which 'I' is taken as equal to but yet not the same as 'thou' and that this again is only possible by putting the 'I' and 'thou' in opposition to each other—in logical antithesis I mean—as correspondent opposites, as harmonies or correlatives." Coleridge, *Opus Maximum*, 12.

us as a nothing, which in turn means that their own self, the self of the other facing me, is extinguished. Unfortunately, this has happened time and again in human history, when one people group sees another nation or race as less than fully equal. One may cite the Rwanda genocide, or Srebrenica as cases in point. Both forms of failure to be conformed to the pattern of humanity that Christ gives us have a significant shame component. When "I–You" becomes "o–You," then I see myself as a person of no intrinsic value. It is a shame assessment. Alternatively, if "I–You" becomes "I–It," then I, as the subject, am guilty of reducing my fellow human being to nothing, in fact I am shaming them.

Whilst this lightning tour of the history of sin in Christian thought has delineated the contours of the nature of sin, we need to explore how the terms "shame" and "guilt" are related to each other in biblical narratives and how both depict facets of "sin." The Bible offers us a range of stories in which both shame and guilt are depicted. In some instances there is a portrayal of shame that is entirely unconnected to guilt. Reference has already been made to the story of Hannah in 1 Sam 1:1–18. Her distress at her barrenness was compounded by the scorn that was heaped upon her by Elkanah's other wife, Peninnah, who intentionally sought to irritate her by reminding her of her inability to bear children. In doing so Peninnah continually reinforced the deep feelings of shame that Hannah was obliged to endure. In Hannah's case her shame was an external imposition, laid upon her shoulders by the cultural expectations of her community and intensified by the competitive provocation of the other wife. Her shame was deep and enduring but lacked any relationship with guilt. It was not the consequence of guilt but simply the outworking of the social construct declaring that to be without a child was to fall short of one's humanity and to lack a claim to full belonging within society. As the barren Hannah stood facing the community to which she belonged, she received the overwhelming message that she was simply not good enough. The weight of that imposition was too much for her to bear, hence her anguished prayer in the house of the Lord.

By contrast, the story of Daniel reveals an utterly different perspective on the experience of shame and guilt. Daniel writes from a position of being an exile in a foreign land. The enforced captivity of the Jewish people provoked a theological crisis of epic proportions. How can God's chosen nation become *slaves* once more? How is it possible to lose the promised land, the holy city, and the temple where God reveals himself? How can an ungodly nation triumph over the people of God? Daniel's desperate search for an answer to such troubling questions led him to re-read the prophecy of Jeremiah, in which he discovers that the prophet had announced that this captivity would last for seventy years. This realization provokes a desperate prayer from the lips and the heart of Daniel and he takes it upon himself to stand before Yahweh as a representative of his entire nation, in utter contrition. His prayer is a collective confession, an acknowledgment that as an entire people the Jews had failed to heed the obligations of the covenant and that in so doing they were now reaping the consequences of their stubborn choices.

> We have not listened to your servants the prophets, who spoke in your name to our kings, our princes, and our fathers, and to all the people of the land. Lord, you are righteous, but this day we are covered with shame—the men of Judah and people of Jerusalem and all Israel, both near and far, in all the countries where you have scattered us because of our unfaithfulness to you. O LORD, we and our kings, our princes and our fathers are covered with shame because we have sinned against you. (Dan 9:6–8)

Daniel's prayer reveals a different relationship between guilt and shame in comparison to that of Hannah. For him the experience of shame was directly connected to the guilt of slothful disobedience. It was the natural outworking of failing to listen to the voice of the prophets who had insistently called the nation back to a place of loving, obedient dependence. The resultant feeling of shame, which he so earnestly articulates, is an expression of the loss of connection to the covenant-keeping God. To be in a foreign land without access to the temple was hugely symbolic. It meant that their attachment to the land—God's gift to them—was severed. They had become outsiders, displaced people, those without a home and as such they now dwelt in a place of acute shame. In some ways their experience was similar to Hannah's for she too felt that her barrenness barred her from fully belonging to her own community. Daniel and the other Jewish exiles no longer belonged to the land and there may have also been the creeping doubt that they no longer belonged to Yahweh either. Thus shame powerfully casts doubt on the core existential desire to exist. To be is to belong, and when shame places a question mark over belonging, then almost everything is lost. For those exiles who languished by the rivers of Babylon, the sense of conviction of guilt at their lack of faithfulness quickly became an acute experience of disgrace.

Daniel's tragic prayer offers us the key that unlocks the door to a deeper understanding of the theological dynamic of "sin." If "sin" is understood as an abstract legal category or part of a "theory," then we run the risk of imposing an alien template upon the biblical narratives. The postmodern critique of Christian theology insists that any attempt to construct a unifying theory inevitably results in the imposition of yet another oppressive and potentially violent storyline. It is what Derrida has named as "Greek-think,"[3] the urge to unify and thus to control. It is my view that "sin" is to be understood within its own narrative context, and that context is always relational. For the Hebrews, identity was intimately related to their attachment to Yahweh, who had delivered them from captivity and who had entered into a covenant with them. This covenantal commitment placed God's people in the promised land and gave them the city of Jerusalem as a symbol of God's abiding presence with them. So profound was this covenantal thinking that when there was a disruption to that committed relationship the prophets resorted to the metaphor of marriage to bring the people back to their senses. The prophet Hosea was called to the unenviable task of dramatically re-enacting in his own life the diagnosis of the nation's unfaithfulness. His marriage to a known adulteress proves to be disastrous and was a profoundly painful experience for him. Despite this, the word comes to him, "The LORD said to me, 'Go, show your love to your wife again, though she is loved by another and is an adulteress. Love her as the LORD loves the Israelites, though they turn to other gods'" (Hos 3:1). He invites the people who hear his message to re-frame their perception of God. Sin is not the failure to reach a moral standard; it is the choice to turn one's back on a loving, committed relationship. Could his hearers possibly imagine that the Lord was their "husband" rather than their lawgiver?

It took a while for King David to appreciate this deeply relational, covenantal nature of sin. After his forceful adultery with Bathsheba and his subsequent murder of her husband, David appeared to have little sense of remorse concerning his guilt. It was only after the risky and imaginative intervention of Nathan, recorded for us in 2 Sam 12, that he experienced a sudden awful realization of what he had done. His sense of conviction of

---

3. Quoted in Vanhoozer, "The Atonement in Postmodernity," 367.

guilt was profound and humbling and in his subsequent reflection on this incident, he wrote the poignant Ps 51 in which he declares, "Against you, you only, have I sinned." It is a striking assertion given that his guilt was obviously connected to his inappropriate and invasive behavior against Bathsheba and Uriah. It was guilt that had been incurred because of David's actions against other human beings, yet David knew that his sin was more serious than that for it was against the covenant-keeping God too. Any oppressive action against another person is also a breach in the relationship with God. It is as if God is so intimately connected with his own creation that any "sin" cannot fail to distort and damage our relationship with God as well.

This moves the language of sin, guilt, and shame out of a cold, legal framework altogether. To remain within such a paradigm is to be wedded to the language of obedience within an economy of "exchange." The language of obedience defines a relationship in terms of how well a function has been performed. It is the kind of language that is entirely appropriate within a military setting where lives are at risk and security is paramount. Such language is inappropriate, however, within a marriage, for here intimacy and trust are key. The Hebrew verb *shāma*ʿ, commonly translated as "to obey," actually means "to hear." For the Israelites to truly "hear" the word of the Lord spoken to them meant that a turning of the head was required. One simply had to turn towards the Lord to hear what was being uttered in his name and once a true hearing had taken place in the heart as well as in the ears then genuine faithfulness would surely follow. To hear was to obey.

The economy of "exchange" mentality has, unfortunately, an enduring and profoundly magnetic attraction. It is built on the assumption that there are rewards for services provided and penalties when there is failure to perform. It is the polar opposite of the language of "gift." Two examples may suffice to illustrate this. In the story of the woman caught in adultery in John 8, a story that we will explore more fully in a later chapter, we witness the collision of the world of exchange with the world of gift. The Pharisees wish to execute the woman on the spot, believing that transgression of the law demands immediate retributive punishment. Jesus, whilst not condoning her lifestyle choices, declares that she is not condemned and that there is to be no balancing of the judicial books. She receives forgiveness for her guilt yet this declaration was offered simply as a gift, unearned, undeserved, unexpected. Jesus recognizes that while her guilt was real it need not be accompanied by the further imposition of shame and it could be dealt with from within the economy of excessive generosity. The stunned silence of the Pharisees illustrates how little they had understood the language of excess.

Likewise, the paralytic who was lowered through the roof by his friends received more than he or they had bargained for (Mark 2:1–12). Not only did the man receive his healing, but Jesus also announces that his sins are forgiven. Immediately consternation amongst the observing crowd breaks out. What began as a desperate search for physical healing turns into a theological crisis for his hearers concerning the way in which forgiveness, sin, and guilt could be dealt with. Jesus exceeds expectations by being excessively gracious. In so doing he reveals the profoundly unsettling, disturbing nature of the world of gift and excess.

5

Psychology

THE CENTRAL SQUARE IN the North African city of Tunis is named after a young man called Muhammad Bouazizi. Tunisia has very high
unemployment and Mohammad scraped a meager living by selling fruit
and vegetables in the main market area. On the morning of December
17th, 2010, he was harassed by a female representative of the city who
claimed he had no permit to set up his stall, and during the altercation
that followed the woman slapped him and confiscated some of his goods.
Mohammed, incensed at the public humiliation he had suffered, rushed
to the nearest petrol station, bought some gasoline and set himself afire.
In Arab culture, to be shamed so visibly was more than Mohammed could
endure. His act of self-immolation was a final protest at the frustration of
living in a secretive, oppressive culture and his public shaming. Photos
of his burning body flashed around the country through social network-
ing media and proved to be iconic in galvanizing a popular uprising. He
became an instant hero and his death triggered a political revolution that
culminated in the collapse of the Tunisian government. Such is the psychological force of shame.

The creation account involving Adam and Eve in the garden functions, as we have already noted, in some ways like a stem cell in the human
body. Geneticists know now that stem cells found in the early stages of a
pregnancy are capable of shaping the future disposition and character of
the fully formed human. Genesis 1–3 offers us similar potential. The psy-

chological consequences of the fateful choice of the first pair are plain to see. The propensity to hide or withdraw from community, the inability to trust, and the tendency to shift blame to others are all symptoms of what would now be recognized as the psychological outworkings of a shame experience. The psychological shift that took place was thus a move away from mutuality, vulnerability, and a lifestyle of interdependence towards something that was intrinsically competitive and suspicious. That competitiveness becomes the basis of society in which hierarchy, status, and the quest for honor are paramount and it can take a multitude of different forms. Whether shame is manifested in the desire to withdraw or to hide from oneself and from involvement in society, or whether it adopts the opposite pole and seeks to apportion blame on others, the psychological phenomenon is ultimately the same. Both cases result in the diminution of the self. If Adam and Eve's instinctive response after their transgression was concealment it suggests that this is one of shame's hallmarks. Whenever there is a tendency for one's true self to be obscured or minimized then one could surmise that the root of such behavior is shame. Likewise, whenever there is a tendency to minimize, blame, or scapegoat another, it is likely that the shame cancer is doing its lethal work.

The culture of the first-century world into which Jesus stepped was founded on honor and shame. David deSilva, in his book *Honor, Patronage, Kinship and Purity*, cites Aristotle who, in his book on ethics, assesses the motives of those who are faced with a choice of seeking either honor or pleasure. Those who chose pleasure above honor were considered to be driven by passions and earthly desires, possessing almost an animal-like quality. Those who opted for honor above pleasure had chosen the highest possible good. The first-century Roman statesman and philosopher Seneca confirmed this view when he wrote: "The one firm conviction from which we move to the proof of other points is this: that which is honorable is held dear for no other reason than because it is honorable."[1] The culture of the Mediterranean lands in the first century, like our own, was very varied, with a number of different groups living side by side. The scattered Jewish communities were steeped in their own tradition, which associated honor with wisdom. Once one acquired true wisdom from above, one also acquired honor.[2] Other communities, however, most no-

1. Quoted in deSilva, *Honor, Patronage, Kinship and Purity*, 23.
2. Ibid., 104.

tably those from a Greek culture, developed an entirely alternative system. Honor for them was tied to the performance of certain civic duties or to public displays of oratory. Perhaps the most significant honor was that of being a generous benefactor of the local community. If one had the means to erect a statue or a plinth dedicated to one of the many deities then this not only ensured some degree of stability for society but also gained the donor a great deal of honor. Those who could not participate in this competitive system of patronage could clearly not climb the ladder of social recognition. Those who refused to participate in the practices of paying homage to the plethora of deities were loathed and held in contempt as disturbers of the peace. Such was the culture into which the early church was born, and against which it had to learn to stand.

Western society today has moved a long way from first-century Palestine and the wider Greco-Roman world and some might argue that such competitive practices have long since disappeared. They may linger in Asian societies but European and North American culture is far more pre-occupied with guilt and pleasure than issues of shame and honor. It is my belief that in our present-day context, avoidance of shame and the search for honor are far more prevalent motivators than at first appears. Shame can, and often does, engulf entire nations. Some historians claim, for example, that the Treaty of Versailles, which was signed in 1919 in the aftermath of the First World War, created the conditions whereby the German nation felt shamed in front of the entire world.[3] It was as if the finger of judgment was pointed at Germany alone, while ignoring, somewhat strangely, Austria and Italy, which had also been complicit. This sense of deep humiliation in Germany, accompanied by the feeling that they were a nation that was now barely tolerated within the larger community of Europe, provided fertile ground for the emergence of the National Socialist Movement under the charismatic leadership of Adolf Hitler. The public shaming of Germany contributed to its alienation within the international community. In October 1933, Hitler took the bold step of withdrawing from the League of Nations, after having become frustrated by the Anglo-French insistence that Germany's army should remain restricted in size according to the terms of the Versailles Treaty. This move outside of the auspices of an internationally recognized organization, was made by Hitler on the grounds that "the other pow-

3. E.g., Evans, *The Third Reich in Power.*

ers" had made "unreasonable, humiliating and degrading demands" upon Germany.[4] Hitler had felt the international finger of shame being pointed at the German nation and it struck a deep wound into its soul. On the evening of the withdrawal from the League of Nations, Hitler delivered a speech in which he outlined the way in which Germany had been deliberately degraded by the international community and had not been granted parity of worth in the negotiations. This public shaming could not and would not be tolerated any longer, said the Führer, and so this one step of withdrawal from international scrutiny and accountability became the dawn of a new and far more aggressive foreign policy. Such is the potency of shame. The legacy of those Nazi dominated years has itself cast a shadow over present-day Germany, with current generations still feeling the acute shame of the Holocaust years, despite the fact that the vast majority of modern Germans were not even born at the time and that they, as individuals, are actually innocent.

The story of the ancient Chinese practice of footbinding provides a different example of the political dynamic of shame. In his book *The Honor Code*, Kwame Anthony Appiah describes the way in which this oppressive practice was extinguished as a direct result of the interplay between honor and shame. When China became drawn more fully into the community of nations and global communication networks improved, this ancient practice was reported around the world, arousing horror and indignation. In Chinese culture the maintenance of honor in the public arena is critically important and once it became known globally that footbinding was being practiced, China ran the risk of enduring the censure of other nations. Appiah records a memorandum which was sent to the Chinese Emperor at the end of the nineteenth century in which he insists that cessation of the practice is a matter of national honor and therefore of the greatest urgency. Here is an excerpt of the letter:

> It is no longer the time when we were united under one rule and isolated from the rest of the world. Now China is narrow and crowded, has opium addicts and streets lined with beggars. Foreigners have been taking pictures and laughing at us for these things and criticizing us for being barbarians. There is nothing

4. Ibid., 618.

> which makes us objects of ridicule so much as foot-binding. I,
> your humble servant, feel deeply ashamed at heart.[5]

Four years later the Emperor issued an edict urging the end of foot-binding.

Not only does shame engulf an entire nation; it is also a profoundly personal, individual affair. The distinguished psychologist James Fowler, who is perhaps best known for his work on the stages of faith development in children, offers a fivefold typology of shame. In his book *Faithful Change: The Personal and Public Challenges of Postmodern Life*, he provides definitions of all five.

1. *Healthy shame* is found where there is a healthy acknowledgment of one's own responsibility. It functions as an early warning system signaling that one's own worth, or that of another, may be placed in danger, possibly leading to a diminution of self-respect.

2. *Perfectionist shame* depicts the experience of an individual who may seek to cover up a deep-seated feeling of unworthiness through persistent perfectionist behavior. It manifests itself in a desire to meet the expectations of others through conformity to certain accepted values and a high emphasis on performance.

3. *Racial-, social-, or gender-based shame* is caused by an enforced, externally imposed minority identity. This expression of shame is one that is imposed by one dominant group upon a perceived lesser group. It can be connected with ethnicity or gender or language or indeed any kind of identification.

4. *Toxic shame* is caused by the abusive and invasive actions of another. This often, but not always, takes place at times of acute vulnerability. Whenever there is radical dislocation between the private and the public self, then it is likely that toxic shame will find fertile soil. Those who have suffered the violence of sexual abuse and subsequently feel the urgent need to hide that abuse from the wider world, know all too well the torment of toxic shame.

5. *Shamelessness* is the final category in Fowler's schema and is the one that he considers to be the most unhealthy of all types of shame. It is found when a person or group feels no conscience or remorse at all when inflicting violence upon others.

5. Appiah, *The Honor Code*, 60.

With the exception of healthy shame, all of the types listed above involve the hiding or the withdrawing of the true self. This withdrawal may be manifested in a physical withdrawal from others, an actual distancing, or it may be a withdrawal from oneself, an overwhelming terror at the prospect of being confronted with the utter ugliness of one's own life. Ultimately it is also a withdrawal from God, fearing that God too would disapprove if he was "allowed" to see all the gory mess that shame produces. This was the first instinctive action of the original couple in the book of Genesis. The desire to hide, to withdraw, and to obscure one's true self is a core component of the experience of shame. The fear is that if one's true nature is transparently clear for all to see, then one runs the risk of being scorned, humiliated, and ultimately rejected.

Perhaps one of its most pervasive features is the fear or anxiety caused by the threat of exposure. This exposure takes the form of one's failings or weaknesses being made manifest in the public arena. It is the fear of having failed to meet both the expectations that one has placed upon oneself and the failure to meet the demands of the society to which one belongs. In both cases the fear that this failure might be seen for what it is causes an experience of shame. Such shame is the root of intense anxiety. Helen Merrell Lynd, in her book *On Shame and the Search for Identity*, articulates the element of exposure that characterizes shame. "Experiences of shame appear to embody the root meaning of the word—to uncover, to expose, to wound. They are experiences of exposure, exposure of particularly sensitive, intimate, vulnerable aspects of the self."[6] Naturally such experiences of shameful anxiety have their own consequences. The shamed one feels alienated from herself or himself, from the wider community, and ultimately from God. It is highly disruptive of all kinds of relationships and it is not hard to envisage how such shame can also lead to real guilt if the alienation is acted out. The trouble with shame is that it often does not have an obvious starting point in contrast to guilt. The experience of guilt is associated with the transgression of a law or an instruction. Once this misdemeanor has taken place there is a clear and obvious ground, a legal case even, for declaring that such a person is "guilty." Guilt and forgiveness naturally live together as counterparts in the same situation. If a guilty person is declared forgiven, the guilt is removed and one can return to a state of contented equilibrium. Shame by contrast is far more sinis-

6. Lynd, *On Shame and the Search for Identity*, 27.

ter. There may be no known conscious cause, but instead a deep-seated malaise that something is wrong. It is not so much the experience that "I have done something bad" but rather "I am bad, existentially, simply by me being myself." It is an experience or a condition that raises a question mark over our right to *be*. It is because of the tangled depth of shame that the simple statement that "in Christ all is forgiven" is unlikely to resonate. Shame does not respond to legal solutions.

A search for the origins of shame in our ordinary human existence was a quest undertaken by the influential psychologist Erik Erikson in his groundbreaking book *Identity and the Life Cycle*, published in 1959. Erikson claims that in each stage of life there are binary polarities in the psychological realm that need to be negotiated. The earliest is the question of Trust versus Mistrust and occurs in the first few months of life as an infant learns to bond with its parents. The second stage of development that contributes to the development of identity Erikson defined as the struggle between Autonomy and Shame. In this stage, which typically characterizes early childhood, the issue of the emergence of a healthy sense of self, a self capable of making sense of the world and taking decisions, is defined as "autonomy." When this natural healthy process is disturbed by inappropriate parenting involving humiliating techniques, then shame is the outcome rather than a self-image. This is how Erikson depicts shame. "Shame supposes that one is completely exposed and conscious of being looked at—in a word, self-conscious. One is visible and not ready to be visible; that is why we dream of shame as a situation in which we are stared at in a condition of incomplete dress, in night attire 'with one's pants down.' Shame is early expressed in an impulse to bury one's face, or to sink, right then and there into the ground."[7] What Erikson had unearthed was none other than the crippling fear of exposure and the accompanying urge to run for cover that we have already delineated in the Genesis story of creation.

Baker and Green in their book *Recovering the Scandal of the Cross* illustrate the psychological dynamic of a shame-based culture by considering the example of Japanese society, as interpreted by the American missionary Norman Kraus, who worked there for many years. They write:

> In a shame-based culture like Japan, public exposure and exclusion are important means for regulating social behavior. A prison

7. Erikson, *Identity and the Life Cycle*, 71.

term, commonly quite long, is not viewed as penal equivalency or rehabilitation but as a way of excluding someone from society. These sanctions work effectively because social relationships are of paramount importance. People place a premium on "saving face." Kraus reports that while he was in Japan a man was released from prison when, after twenty years, his innocence came to light. Upon his release, he first went to his father's grave and told his father that the family shame had been resolved.[8]

Whilst this Japanese prisoner had experienced the full force of the judicial system, the purpose of his imprisonment was not punitive in the same sense that prison is used as a means of social control in the West. Rather, in Japan a custodial sentence is intended to impose a period of public shaming, exposure, and loss of face, with the intention that ultimately such shame may be removed and the criminal be allowed to re-integrate into society once more.

The tragic events of the Balkan wars of the 1990s point to this very tendency. Once the Soviet Empire had begun to crumble, Yugoslavia, ruled for decades by President Tito, began to disintegrate. In the chaos that ensued, different ethnic groups began to minimize, blame, and scapegoat each other. The Serbian incursion into Croatia and the attempted ethnic cleansing of Croats from the capital Sarajevo resulted in huge loss of life and widespread trauma. The Croatian theologian Miroslav Volf was then faced with a deeply personal, psychological, and theological dilemma. What was to be his attitude towards those who had committed such atrocities? In the preface to his book *Exclusion and Embrace* he writes about an experience of delivering a lecture on reconciliation and forgiveness. "It was the winter of 1993. For months now the notorious Serbian fighters called 'cetnik' had been sowing desolation in my native country, herding people into concentration camps, raping women, burning down churches, and destroying cities. I had just argued (in a lecture) that we ought to embrace our enemies as God has embraced us in Christ."[9] At the conclusion of his lecture the German theologian Jürgen Moltmann, who had been listening attentively, asked him a devastatingly simple question. "Can you, as a Croat, embrace a cetnik (a Serb)"? Volf continues, "Can I embrace a 'cetnik'—the ultimate other, so to speak, the evil other? What

8. Green and Baker, *Recovering the Scandal of the Cross*, 159.

9. Volf, *Exclusion and Embrace*, 9.

would justify the embrace? Where would I draw the strength for it? What would it do to my identity as a human being and as a Croat?" It was then that Volf realized that in reality he could not embrace a "cetnik," for the feelings of hatred and revulsion ran so deep. Yet after reflection he went on to write, "No, I cannot—but as follower of Christ I think I should be able to."[10]

Volf's experience illustrates the psychological circularity of shame and its connection with guilt. What began with the shaming of one nation (the Croats) by another (the Serbs) resulted in the powerful temptation to reciprocate by an equal and opposite act of shaming. The Serbs now deserve to be minimized, belittled, and shamed in return. In recognizing the demonic attractiveness of this option, Volf sought to rebuild a theology that escaped from this deadly cycle and enabled him to see "the other" standing before him not as an enemy, nor a competitor, nor as a nothing, but as person or a nation also made in the image of God. To live in a world without the "other" is to deny one of the essential trinity of "otherness" that we have already explored. A world without otherness can lead to a frightening homogeneity, a doorway to ethnic purity. The twentieth century was tragically filled with attempts to live without "the other."

The tendency to resort to blame is part of the psychological dynamic of scapegoating that often accompanies experiences of shame. To blame another for one's own exposure is a convenient way of avoiding responsibility for one's own actions. It shifts the focus of attention away from the self and the perceived threat to that self and places it firmly upon the shoulders of another. This dynamic is vividly illustrated in the story of King Saul and his dealings with his son Jonathan, who developed a close personal friendship with the man that Saul considered to be his archenemy—David. We pick up the story in 1 Sam 20.

> Saul's anger flared up at Jonathan and he said to him, "You son of a perverse and rebellious woman! Don't I know that you have sided with the son of Jesse to your own shame and to the shame of the mother who bore you? As long as the son of Jesse lives on this earth, neither you nor your kingdom will be established. Now send someone to bring him to me, for he must die!" "Why should he be put to death? What has he done?" Jonathan asked his father. But Saul hurled his spear at him to kill him. Then Jonathan knew that his father intended to kill David. Jonathan got up from the

10. Ibid.

table in fierce anger; on that second day of the feast he did not eat, because he was grieved at his father's shameful treatment of David. (1 Sam 20:30–34)

The way in which this narrative unfolds reveals a highly toxic chain of events. It may be helpful to list the sequence numerically.

1. Although Saul is king, his position appears to him to be under threat from the increasingly popular young pretender, David.

2. King Saul arranges a New Moon festival to which he invites both David and his own son Jonathan.

3. After two days, David, who fears for his own life, does not appear at the king's table, thereby publicly inflicting shame on the king. How could an invited guest not appear at the royal banquet?

4. Saul suspects that David's non-appearance must have something to do with Jonathan who is perceived to be in a close and collusive relationship with David.

5. Saul explodes in fury when he hears Jonathan's lame explanation for David's absence and begins to hurl accusations at his son.

6. He calls his own wife, Jonathan's mother, a "perverse and rebellious woman." Some commentators claim that this kind of description is tantamount to calling her a whore.[11] He therefore shames her in public, and, in that culture, it was believed that shame was transmitted genetically through the mother. Thus, if Jonathan's mother was depicted as a whore, it automatically meant that Jonathan too was disgraced.

7. Jonathan's close friendship with David means that his own claim to the throne of Saul is immediately invalidated, thereby bringing shame both on himself and his father.

8. The phrase that is translated here as "and to the shame of the mother who bore you" is more accurately rendered, as in the King James Version, as "and unto the confusion of thy mother's nakedness." It was as if Jonathan's actions in colluding with David had shamefully exposed the nakedness of his own mother.

---

11. Stansell, "Honor and Shame in the David Narratives," 60.

9. The story reaches its climax when Saul insists that David must surely die (v. 31) and calls him *ben-māwet* (literally "son of death"). The spear that was hurled at Jonathan symbolically means death for David too. Jonathan leaves the feast in furious anger because his father has engaged him a series of shaming and blaming actions.

In his refusal to take responsibility for his own increasingly bizarre and desperate behavior, Saul lashes out in blame. It is the fault of David, it is the fault of his own son Jonathan, and it is even the fault of his own wife. All are named and shamed. It is a truly toxic event illustrating the scapegoating dynamic of shame and it proves to be pivotal in the unfolding drama of the nation. In time Saul loses all legitimacy to govern and is replaced by David. In the economy of God the violent cycle of blame is not victorious, for David becomes king and is known as "a man after God's own heart." It is through David that some measure of restoration occurs within the life of God's people and it is through David that the promised Messiah would eventually come. The narrative pre-figures the way in which Jesus, the son of David, would one day absorb and nullify a final, ultimate scapegoating.

6

Spirituality

THE CREATION STORY, WITH which we began, illustrated Adam and Eve
hiding from God in the aftermath of their transgression. This desire to
become invisible to the searching gaze of God is one of the spiritual hallmarks of shame. It demonstrates how shame skews and alters our perception of the nature of God's character. Before they had eaten the forbidden
fruit, they had no doubts about the loving orientation of God towards
them, yet afterwards this same God is perceived in an entirely new way.
His face is to be *avoided*, his intentions to be *doubted*, his presence to
be *shunned*. No less is true for us today. Martin Luther astutely observed
that the essence of sin was precisely this inward curve of the human heart
upon itself, instead of its being open to the fullness of God's grace. The
prophet Isaiah perceptively notices the tendency towards shame in his
own society. Those who had lived a reckless life in their youth still carried
within them the memory of those shameful experiences in their souls.
For them it felt like a weight of disgrace and those women who had suffered the loss of their husbands knew for themselves how difficult it was
to thrive in a society when one lacked a male provider. Widowhood had
become for them a reproach. To all such people who lived under the burden of shame Isaiah declared the word of the Lord, announcing that he
would remove their disgrace, he would become their husband, he would
turn his face towards them once more.

> Do not be afraid; you will not suffer shame. Do not fear disgrace;
> you will not be humiliated. You will forget the shame of your youth
> and remember no more the reproach of your widowhood. For
> your Maker is your husband—the LORD Almighty is his name—
> the Holy One of Israel is your Redeemer; he is called the God of
> all the earth. The LORD will call you back as if you were a wife
> deserted and distressed in spirit—a wife who married young, only
> to be rejected, says your God. For a brief moment I abandoned
> you, but with deep compassion I will bring you back. In a surge
> of anger I hid my face from you for a moment, but with everlast-
> ing kindness I will have compassion on you, says the LORD your
> Redeemer. (Isa 54:4–8)

Without hearing this liberating voice, shamed people develop an impoverished spirituality. It is a centripetal one, if indeed it is a spirituality at
all, centered entirely and destructively upon oneself. It bears a number of
distinctive hallmarks.

Hiding

Luke's Gospel records the calling of the first disciples and includes a tale
about Peter's encounter with Jesus in his fishing boat. Having fished all
night and caught nothing, Jesus invites Peter to push the boat out once
more. Peter, the professional fisherman, naturally objects to the apparently absurd suggestion. Fishing is best done at night, not in broad day-
light. Yet eventually he agrees and to his astonishment a huge catch of fish
is caught. Upon observing the extraordinary haul of fish in unexpected
circumstances Peter cries out to Jesus, "Depart from me, for I am a sinful man" (Luke 5:8). What cognitive and emotional processes took place
within Peter between his observation of bulging fishing nets and his subsequent outburst? One is left to surmise that he concluded that if Jesus
knew the exact whereabouts of a hidden shoal of fish lying in the deep,
then he would also know the secrets lying deep in his own heart. Peter
could not bear to contemplate such exposure, hence his immediate desire
to hide.

Likewise, the parable of the talents depicts a person caught up in a
fearful cycle of shame. He had been given gifts by his master to use to the
full in whatever way he chose to. The master goes away on a journey and
on his return summons the servant to give account of himself. "Then the

man who had received the one talent came. 'Master,' he said, 'I knew that you are a hard man, harvesting where you have not sown and gathering where you have not scattered seed. So I was afraid and went out and hid your talent in the ground. See, here is what belongs to you'" (Matt 25:14). The fact that those talents were hidden from view and therefore unused showed a basic level of mistrust towards his master. He feared that the re-action he would receive would be more than he could bear and his imme-diate response was to hide. His anxiety turned around the question of how the master was perceived. Here was a man who had displayed confidence and trust in his servants, yet he was viewed as being entirely other than this—harsh, mean, judgmental. In the face of such a person, the servant opted to hide in the vain hope that this choice would never be exposed.

The theologian Paul Tillich once preached a sermon that was based on the beautiful Ps 139, which speaks of God's utter and complete knowledge of us. In his sermon Tillich makes reference to the writings of the ardent atheist Friedrich Nietzsche who wrote the novel *Thus Spoke Zarathustra*. Tillich was aware that God's searching gaze is not always welcome, especially to those who are conscious of their shame. He writes,

> Friedrich Nietzsche, the famous atheist and ardent enemy of re-ligion and Christianity, knew more about the power of the idea of God than many faithful Christians. In a symbolic story, when Zarathustra, the prophet of a higher humanity, says to the Ugliest Man, the murderer of God, "You could not bear him to see you, always to see you through and through . . . You took revenge on the witness . . . You are the murderer of God." The Ugliest Man agrees with Zarathustra and replies, "He had to die." For God, according to the Ugliest Man, looks with eyes that see everything; He peers into man's ground and depth, into his hidden shame and ugliness. The God who sees everything, and man also, is the God who has to die. Man cannot stand that such a Witness live.

For Nietzsche the continual desire to hide from God's presence can only be satisfied by the death of God, rather than by falling into his embrace.

Exposure

The threat of being shamed is a repeated refrain for the Psalm writers. It is as if the most serious form of exposure and public humiliation is the possibility of being placed in a position of utter shame. "To you, O lord, I lift up my soul," writes David. "O my God, in you I have trust, let me not be ashamed" (Ps 25:1–2). In these kinds of petitions, the psalmist claims that he has explicitly and publicly put his trust in Yahweh, thereby exposing him to the risk of being taunted or mocked by others less devout than himself. He therefore cries to the Lord that he would not suffer humiliation and shame in the eyes of his adversaries. This fear of being shamed remains a constant threat. Hear for example these cries from the heart.

> "O keep my soul, and deliver me. Let me not be ashamed; for I put my trust in thee" (Ps 25:20).

> "In thee, O LORD, do I put my trust; let me never be ashamed. Deliver me in thy righteousness" (Ps 31:1).

> "Let me not be ashamed, O LORD; for I have called upon thee. Let the wicked be ashamed, and let them be silent in the grave" (Ps 31:17).

These passionate cries reveal a genuine fear that one could lose face within the community and suffer mocking and taunting that would be unbearable. To endure such torment either from within the community of Israel or from those seemingly arrogant neighboring nations, was, for the psalmist, to enter a place of shame. Hence the urgent petitions. Psalm 119 opens with the declaration, "Blessed are they whose ways are blameless, who walk according to the law of the LORD. Blessed are they who keep his statutes and seek him with all their heart . . . Then I would not be put to shame when I consider all your commands." John Goldingay, in his commentary on the book of Psalms, offers this alternative rendering: "The good fortune of people of integrity in their way of life, who walk in Yhwh's teaching! The good fortune of people who observe his declarations, who have recourse to him with all their heart . . . then I shall not be ashamed as I look on all your commands."[1] These opening verses contrast two vastly different conditions of states of being. The first is found in verses 1 and 2: The people who are truly blessed are those who enjoy good fortune. This refers not only to being prosperous and healthy but perhaps more importantly to being held in a place of honor in a community that respects people of integrity. The counterpart to this position of good fortune, the opposite of being blessed, is to be shamed. This shaming occurs when the

---

1. Goldingay, *Psalms*, 381.

refusal to walk in the way of the Lord leads inevitably to a secure position within the community being placed in jeopardy or in some way compromised. Blessing and shaming are held in parallel in this psalm, with one being the opposite of the other. For the devout Jew it would be impossible to conceive of a more dire position to be in than a place of shame.

Perhaps this is why, at moments of the most acute distress, with adversaries seemingly around every corner, the psalmist's desire for justice to be meted out to his adversaries is articulated as a longing for divine shaming. The psalmist asks that the Lord would vindicate his faith by shaming his opponents. Psalm 35, for example, calls on Yahweh for face-saving vindication: "Let them be shamed and humiliated who seek my life, let them be turned back and disgraced who plan my calamity . . . Let them be ashamed and disgraced together who rejoice at my calamity! Let them be clothed with shame and humiliation who magnify themselves against me!" Here God is the subject of the act of shaming, suggesting that God's shaming is connected to both his judgment and to a sense of disclosure. By shaming the opponents of the psalmist, God is making plain their deceit and hypocrisy for all to see. The psalmist is not so much demanding revenge but rather that the falsehood and duplicity of his enemies be recognized as such.

Divine Abandonment

The converse of this human tendency to hide is fear that God himself might hide his face, or at least appear to do so. This is one of the fears repeatedly expressed in the Psalms and is described as the experience of divine abandonment. It is as if God has failed to keep his part of the deal and has let the psalmist down. Psalm 89 is a royal psalm where the writer feels that Yahweh has not fulfilled his covenantal responsibilities to the house of David: "You have rejected, you have spurned, you have been very angry with your anointed one. You have renounced the covenant with your servant and have defiled [shamed] his crown in the dust . . . You have cut short the days of his youth, you have covered him with a mantle of shame" (Ps 89:38–39, 45). The shame which was inflicted on the king was not as a result of guilt, or lack of obedience; it was simply the result of the feeling of divine abandonment. The king had placed his trust in Yahweh but had appeared foolish. It looked as if his trust had been misplaced.

One of the most vivid and tortured examples of the spirituality of shame can be observed in the experience of exile. The wholesale defeat of the kingdom of Judah and the deportation of a significant number of its population to Babylon in 587 BC provoked, unsurprisingly, a crisis. It was a crisis of national identity and theological despair. How can we, God's chosen people to whom such wonderful and seemingly unchangeable promises have been given, find ourselves in a foreign land away from the very place where God had put his name? If God is our rock, then why has the rock moved? Are his promises invalid now? It is hard to imagine the depths of confusion and agonized desperation that the exiles must have endured. For seventy years they were, both geographically and spiritually, in a place of the deepest shame and it is out of these depths that Ps 137 emerges. "By the rivers of Babylon we sat and wept when we remembered Zion. There on the poplars we hung our harps, for there our captors asked us for songs, our tormentors demanded songs of joy; they said, 'Sing us one of the songs of Zion!' How can we sing the songs of the LORD while in a foreign land?" Not only were they sitting beside an unknown river in a strange land but now their captors heap further humiliation upon them. "Sing!" they demand, "we wish to hear your songs of joy!" These are the taunts of the victors shaming their victims gleefully. The response of these exiles is, at first, silence. Their voices of praise are rendered dumb for this is the outworking of shame, a condition and an experience that silences any form of doxology. It is shame that makes their souls shrink; they are now the powerless, the voiceless, the hopeless. All they can do is wait for their exile to end.

Yet in that place of exile two other aspects of shame spirituality gradually emerge. One is the determination, the deliberate choice, to *remember*. Even though they were in an acutely painful place, devoid of meaning and purpose, one thing that they could choose to do was to remember, to picture in their imaginations the holy city of Jerusalem, the place that they associated with greatest joy. "If I forget you, O Jerusalem, may my right hand forget its skill. May my tongue cling to the roof of my mouth if I do not remember you, if I do not consider Jerusalem my highest joy." It was there that they remembered how they met with God. That memory could never be erased for the experience of God's presence was so profound, so immanent. Yet that same remembering leads inexorably to another form of remembering. This time it is the memory of abuse and terror.

"Remember, O LORD, what the Edomites did on the day Jerusalem fell. 'Tear it down,' they cried, 'tear it down to its foundations!'" They replay those dreadful events when they were surrounded and unable to defend themselves any longer. They remember the cries of the advancing hordes, screaming for destruction. They remember all too vividly the invasive moment of their greatest shame. As they bring to mind these violations, a rage wells up within them. How could these strangers have done this to us? How dare they? And from the depths this rage issues forth in a desire for the most violent revenge. "O Daughter of Babylon, doomed to destruction, happy is he who repays you for what you have done to us—he who seizes your infants and dashes them against the rocks."

It is as if a button has been pressed and an emotional eruption unleashed. Those who have been shamed may well be able to resonate with the writer of Ps 137 at this point. When one has been the recipient of "toxic shame," to use the words of Fowler, it is not uncommon to find a reservoir of rage lurking deep within. For some, this rage is so intense and so frightening it is easier to simply deny that it exists at all. It remains locked away in an interior room of the soul unacknowledged and repressed. Yet those who know this will be conscious that their response to situations of fresh humiliation—even if these are imaginary—often elicit a rage out of all proportion to the event that acts as a trigger. Something has touched that wounded spot and unleashed a rage that may feel primeval in its intensity. Yet, whilst Ps 137 illustrates the spirituality of exilic shame, it does not ultimately leave us in utter, total despair. The silencing, the humiliation, and the rage are all expressed and offered to God. They do not remain hidden from view and are articulated in their raw authenticity. In the place of apparent abandonment God is still present and able to hear the anguished cries of the shamed. It is to God that these petitions are offered in the knowledge that, despite the hopelessness of the circumstances, God can still be trusted.

7

Body

THE REFERENCE TO NAKEDNESS in the Genesis account of creation is, as we have noted, no incidental piece of trivia. It is included in the story to demonstrate that the original state of innocence was not something mystical, but rather was characterized by a genuine physicality. When Adam first spied Eve, it was her body that he admired—"bone of my bones and flesh of my flesh," he said. This was no disembodied companion for him, but rather something beautiful, touchable, and honorable. So any theology of the body must begin with the theology of Creation and not with the Fall. Our bodies are an integral, vital part of the creative pattern and when the original couple gazed at one another unclothed there was a complete absence of any shame. The story of their subsequent experience of turning away from the express desire of God for them illustrates that there was an essential physical dimension to this shameful episode. The immediate, instinctive desire was to cover their bodies, to nullify them, thereby rendering them insignificant. It was as if the very act of eating—a physical action involving biting, salivating, swallowing, and ingesting—appeared to be the source of some kind of bodily pollution. The dreadful deed was performed through the body and remembered by the body. Thus the body became one more aspect of the divided self. It was no longer something beautiful to behold for now it had become the enemy, to be locked away, hidden behind a covering.

Yet there is no escape from the body, for our bodies are part of who we are and the shame that is carried in our souls is also carried in our bodies. Those who have been shamed by another—whether that "other" be an individual or a society—will appreciate all too well the truth of this assertion. Shame is often felt as a real sensation in the body. It is as if the experiences of life are stored within our own physical selves and not merely in the mind. It is not uncommon for victims of abuse to experience shame as a bodily felt sense, which is almost impossible to articulate in words. The shame is likened to a foreign object, something alien, alive perhaps, but with the smell of death about it. It has its own separate yet toxic existence within the physical being of the sufferer. The body is aware of the presence of this intruder but is helpless to expel it or deal with its awful effects.

In an earlier chapter we noted the comment of Dietrich Bonhoeffer, who remarked that the fall of mankind revealed a deep shame at the loss of unity with God and with others. Shame is an expression of separation, division, the tearing apart of that which was always intended to be held together in harmonious beauty. One aspect of that splitting is the distortion within the individual in relation to his or her own physicality.

Two related but opposite tendencies become evident. One is the idolizing of the body, seen in countless images and iconic figures who apparently have the perfect body that we all desire. This exaltation of the body into a place of worship is profoundly narcissistic and yet perversely, at its root, manifests a sense of dissatisfaction with and alienation from the body. At the other end of the spectrum, a disdain for the body, tragically observed in those with eating disorders, speaks of an uneasy, uncomfortable relationship with one's own physicality. The body becomes the enemy against which we must daily beware. Attitudes towards the human body, however, vary enormously across cultures and render interpretation of cultural practices a highly sensitive issue. The wearing of a burkha in some Islamic countries is viewed within such cultures as a means of protecting the female body from prying male eyes. Yet from another perspective it is seen as a form of male oppression and domination. Rites of passage involving circumcision or body scarring are considered by some to be necessary actions to ensure an enduring sense of identity, yet for others they are simply a form of brutalization.

Over the centuries the Christian church has struggled to formulate an adequate theology of the body. Influenced perhaps by the prevailing paradigms of Greek philosophy, the early church quickly tended to become suspicious of the body. By way of example, the Council of Carthage, which was convened in 390 AD, issued this canonical rule regarding the ordination of bishops and priests:

> Canon 3: It is fitting that the holy bishops and priests of God as well as the Levites, i.e., those who are in the service of the divine sacraments, observe perfect continence, so that they may obtain in all simplicity what they are asking from God; what the Apostles taught and what antiquity itself observed, let us also endeavor to keep . . . It pleases us all that bishop, priest, and deacon, guardians of purity, abstain from conjugal intercourse with their wives, so that those who serve at the altar may keep a perfect chastity.[1]

This early ecclesiastical ruling illustrates how sexual relations, even within marriage, were seen as a distraction and a hindrance to the service of God. This is expressed very vividly too in the lives of the Desert Fathers who practiced extreme forms of asceticism and bodily deprivation. Anthony of Egypt is known to have entered his desert cell to remain in silent stillness before God. Yet in that cell he encountered hordes of demons knocking incessantly on the door, intent on tempting him away from devotion to God through the pleasures of the flesh.

Developing a Christian theology of the body was part of the challenge facing the great fourth-century theologian of North Africa, Augustine of Hippo. He sought to come to terms with the Christian faith, which he appropriated for himself in adult life, and his earlier exposure to Platonism. The good news of the gospel was announced into a Graeco-Roman culture that had been shaped by centuries of Platonic attitudes to the body. Plato's Theory of Forms had been foundational in developing a concept that declared that the material world that we can see, handle, and physically experience in so many ways was inferior to the higher world of abstract ideas and ideals. This abstract world was the location of the Logos, a hidden force that determined the way in which the universe functioned. The human body, belonging as it so obviously did to the lower sphere of the material, was viewed as the rather inferior housing of the human soul. The task of each individual was to transcend this habitat and to rise

1. http://www.ccel.org/ccel/schaff/npnf214.xv.iv.iv.iv.html.

to a higher plane of existence. It is to people steeped in this Greek philosophical world that John addressed his Gospel with the explosive opening words, "The Word [Greek, *Logos*] became flesh and made his dwelling among us. We have seen his glory, the glory of the one and only Son, who came from the Father, full of grace and truth" (John 1:14). This dramatic announcement at the beginning of John's Gospel—that the eternal Word, the Logos, has actually *become flesh*—is a declaration of the intrinsic value that God places on our weak, frail, and vulnerable human bodies. If the Son of God can willingly inhabit a body, then they must be of infinite worth.

Despite the radically subversive nature of the opening lines of John's Gospel, the conclusion that Augustine reached appeared to demonstrate a reluctance to leave Greek philosophy altogether.[2] He asserted that whilst the human being was a composite of both body and soul it remained the task of the soul to rule the body. It was not therefore a mutual, symmetrical relationship, and this view clearly carried vestiges of his Neo-Platonism. For Augustine, the soul was housed in the body, rather than trapped within it. The body was not the enemy from which the soul must escape, but neither was it an equal partner. Such an attitude betrays an approach to the body that is less than enthusiastic, and this slight ambivalence has, no doubt, influenced later theological developments.

In the light of these historical developments it is surprising perhaps to find that the biblical evidence demands a more rounded, wholesome approach to the body and this is particularly important in its relationship to shame. If we trace the development of attitudes to the body in the Old Testament it is possible to observe a swift departure from the innocent naïveté illustrated in the creation story. By the time the narrative reaches the account of Noah and his sons in Gen 9, public displays of nakedness are a source of the most acute shame. Noah is recorded one day as having too many glasses of his homemade wine. The inevitable inebriation that followed resulted in him being seen lying in his tent, unconscious, with his genitals exposed. Even the careful attempt of his sons to cover him does not stem his acute shame such that on waking from his sleep he resorts to cursing (Gen 9:18–28). The Hebrew word that is used in this narrative for Noah lying "uncovered" is *gālâ*, a word that means to

2. Cf. Augustine, *De Animae Quantitate* 13:22; Augustine, *De Genesi contra Manicheos* II.11.

"shamelessly uncover," to "expose," and to "drive into exile." The reason for the exilic reference is that in Old Testament times, if captives were being taken away to a foreign land, they were routinely stripped naked and chained together. The record of the deportation of the northern kingdom of Israel to Assyria in 2 Kgs 18, for example, states that "the king of Assyria deported [*gālâ*] Israel to Assyria and settled them in Halah, in Gozan on the Habor River and in towns of the Medes."

There is a deep linguistic and cultural connection therefore between the uncovering of a person's nakedness, causing shame, and the experience of exile. By the time of Isaiah's prophetic utterances against the threat of the mighty Babylonian empire, the expression of the judgment of God was couched in terms of the exposure of nakedness, causing the most distressing experience of shame. One can sense the fearlessness of Isaiah as he declares to the Babylonians: "Your nakedness will be exposed and your shame uncovered. I will take vengeance; I will spare no one" (Isa 47:3). The naked exposure of the body has now become a sign of a curse, the judgment of God poured out in full measure. Perhaps that is what Paul had in mind in his letter to the Romans when he writes to the churches in Rome, a city preoccupied with issues of shame and honor, "Who shall separate us from the love of Christ? Shall trouble or hardship or persecution or famine or *nakedness* or danger or sword?" (Rom 8:35). How could nakedness be listed as a possible means by which one can become separated from the love of Christ? Only if the public and perhaps enforced exposure of the human body had come to symbolize the deeply held cultural value of shame. And if one was shamed one was intrinsically cut off from the love of Christ.

The ancient Hebrews were well aware of the deeply physical and psychological aspect of human existence and located such emotional experiences in the bowels, the stomach, the kidneys, and the uterus. The Hebrew word for this place was *rāḥam* and it was used whenever a keenly felt emotion was being experienced. The story of Joseph and his brothers in the book of Genesis illustrates this well. Towards the conclusion of the story, we read of Joseph meeting his younger brother Benjamin for the first time, after many years of tragic separation. The narrator builds up the tension of the story until it reaches its denouement when Joseph sees his youngest brother once more. Genesis 43:30 records the event: "*Deeply moved* at the sight of his brother, Joseph hurried out and looked for a place to weep." The literal translation of the Hebrew at this point is "when his bowels [*raḥămāyw*] grew warm"(!), meaning that he was moved with great compassion. In similar fashion when the prophet Jeremiah could perceive the advancing armies coming to wreak destruction upon the nation, he cries out in despair: "Oh, my anguish, my anguish! I writhe in pain. Oh, the agony of my heart! My heart pounds within me, I cannot keep silent. For I have heard the sound of the trumpet; I have heard the battle cry" (Jer 4:19). The word translated here as "anguish" actually derives from the Hebrew word *mēʿeh* signifying the intestines. The Psalms too contain copious references to the body as the place where shame is experienced and memories are stored. Psalm 31 illustrates the acute pain that the author, King David, feels. He opens his psalm with the acknowledgment that he has taken refuge in God, precisely because he is desperate to avoid being shamed by his enemies. Yet despite this place of security he still feels insecure and disorientated and expresses this in terms of what is happening to his body: "Be merciful to me, LORD, for I am in distress, my eyes grow weak with sorrow, my soul and body with grief. My life is consumed by anguish and my years by groaning, my strength fails because of my affliction, and my bones grow weak" (Ps 31:9–10). Something is happening to his body; his eyes are weakened and filled with tears, his strength begins to fade, and he feels great weakness in his bones. It is as if his whole body is affected by the distress and anguish he is suffering.

In similar vein, New Testament emotional language uses terms that have a resonance with the body. The story of the parable of the prodigal son in Luke 15 depicts the yearning that the father feels for his estranged son. The Greek word *splagchnizomai* denotes great compassion arising from deep within, literally from the spleen and the intestines. It is this word that Luke uses to describe the feelings of the father when he spies his wayward son returning from the far country (Luke 15:20). These word studies only serve to illustrate the way in which the intensely inner experience of shame is recorded and articulated from a deep place within us, a place with which Hebrew spirituality was entirely familiar.

In New Testament times, attitudes toward the body had become the source of much division within society. As Neyrey has pointed out, in the New Testament world, the head and face were the particular loci of honor and respect.[3] A person received honor when his head was crowned and

---

3. Neyrey, *Honor and Shame in the Johannine Passion Narrative*, 117.

when servants approached a king they would avert their eyes to avoid looking directly at the face. So when Jesus was on trial one of the means by which he was shamed was when his tormentors spat in his face, slapped him, and then mockingly crowned him with thorns (Matt 26:27). Similarly bodily postures became highly significant culturally. Those in positions of honor would sit at table and servants would stand. In the light of this, it is all the more significant that at the Last Supper, recorded for us in John 13, Jesus leaves his position of honor and we find him taking the lowly place of shame in order to wash the feet of those at the table with him.

The ministry of Jesus sought to reverse the commonly accepted attitudes to honor and shame expressed through the body, as can be seen, for example, in the story of the healing of the bleeding woman in Mark 5:24–34.

> A large crowd followed and pressed around him. And a woman was there who had been subject to bleeding for twelve years. She had suffered a great deal under the care of many doctors and had spent all she had, yet instead of getting better she grew worse. When she heard about Jesus, she came up behind him in the crowd and touched his cloak, because she thought, "If I just touch his clothes, I will be healed." Immediately her bleeding stopped and she felt in her body that she was freed from her suffering. At once Jesus realized that power had gone out from him. He turned around in the crowd and asked, "Who touched my clothes?" "You see the people crowding against you," his disciples answered, "and yet you can ask, 'Who touched me?'" But Jesus kept looking around to see who had done it. Then the woman, knowing what had happened to her, came and fell at his feet and, trembling with fear, told him the whole truth. He said to her, "Daughter, your faith has healed you. Go in peace and be freed from your suffering."

The Gospel writer, Mark, paints a vivid picture of a woman in distress. She has been suffering from bleeding and has suffered at the hands of various doctors for many years. Levitical tradition demanded that if a woman had an issue of blood she was "unclean" and must remain separate until the bleeding stopped (Lev 15:25ff.).[4] In her case, the bleeding had

---

4. Scholars are divided over the interpretation of the Levitical purity laws in Leviticus 15. The feminist theologian Elizabeth Moltmann-Wendel considers that they are derived from post exilic Judaism and are an androcentric reaction to the earlier gynocentric reverence for fertility and blood. As such they are not particularly Jewish but a composite view drawn from the surrounding Mediterranean cultures. (Moltmann-Wendel, *I am my*

never stopped—for twelve long years—which means that it was a serious, chronic condition, possibly unrelated to any menstrual cycle. It was because of this continuous bleeding that she was effectively ostracized from full participation in the community. She approached Jesus from behind, not wanting to be noticed by anyone lest she suffer the further ignominy of becoming a public spectacle. Yet her desperate lunge was accompanied by the merest flicker of faith, enough to trigger an extraordinary response. She knew instantly that something had taken place in her body, that after all this time her suffering had come to an end. It was her body that had announced to her that a healing had taken place. The reciprocal response from Jesus is likewise located in his body. He knew that something had gone out of him and it was left to the woman to explain the full story of her life. Yet Jesus does not allow the healing to go unnoticed. Her desire for anonymity is not heeded for Jesus stops and deliberately draws the attention of the pressing crowd to this woman. One can only imagine the calculated shock that this would have elicited. Here is a woman who for the past twelve years has lived in the shadows of her community on the margins of society, and now she is the center of attention.

Four aspects of this brief incident are worthy of note. Firstly, it is the woman who approaches Jesus and is permitted to touch him. He does not object to the initiative that she has taken and it appears that in this case the activity of the woman is paired with the passive receptivity of Jesus. It was clearly a huge step for the woman to take and one that involved a high degree of risk. However, to be the initiator of her own recovery may have been an essential part of the process of being healed of her shameful condition. And it may also be true today that those whose bodies have been passive recipients of abusive violation would draw strength from the example of this woman. Taking back some degree of control is part of the process of being healed of shame.

The second facet of this encounter is that Jesus simply calls her "daughter," without any personal pronoun. It is an intimate word, but used here to suggest something other than a father-daughter relationship. It is more likely that Jesus was evoking the text from the prophet Isaiah which reads, "The LORD has made proclamation to the ends of the earth: 'Say to

---

Body, 38). Walter Brueggemann, by contrast, regards the regulations as instruments of the safe ordering of society and that they are not to be understood as making any kind of moral statement (Brueggemann, *Theology of the Old Testament*, 191).

Daughter Zion, See, your Savior comes! See, his reward is with him, and his recompense accompanies him'" (Isa 62:11). The word "daughter," in this prophetic text, refers to the whole nation of Israel. The action of Jesus and his words to the woman, alluding to Isaiah's declaration, announced that healing for the whole people of God, who for so long had suffered the shame of exile, was indeed possible and that such healing would take place in the body for those who have the faith to reach out and touch. As Elisabeth Moltmann-Wendel puts it, "liberation takes place in the body."[5]

Thirdly, Jesus declares to her that she is now healed from her illness and that she can go in peace. The Greek word (*mastix*) that is translated as "plague" in the King James Version and "suffering" in the text quoted above, means literally "a scourge." It was a form of punishment that normally involved a whip and is used by Luke to describe what happened to Paul on his missionary travels (Acts 22:24). The bleeding that the woman had endured was no less a calamity, similar to the Roman practice of flogging criminals, such was the depth of her shame.

Finally, Jesus declares to her that she is now to "go in peace," a phrase that would have evoked the Hebrew word "šālôm," meaning "wholeness." She leaves the scene not only whole in her body but re-integrated into society. The crucial theological significance of this event is that the encounter between Jesus and the shamed woman happened within their bodies and it was through their bodies that healing was communicated.

Another striking story in the Gospels that has a bearing on this issue is told in Mark 7:32–33 and concerns the healing of a deaf man. The setting is a public one in which some people from the crowd bring to Jesus someone who was deaf and therefore also suffering from a speech impediment. "There some people brought to him a man who was deaf and could hardly talk, and they begged Jesus to place his hand on him. After he took him aside, away from the crowd, Jesus put his fingers into the man's ears. Then he spit and touched the man's tongue." The means by which the deaf man was healed was through a bodily fluid, some spittle, from Jesus. To the modern mind using spittle seems somewhat coarse, superstitious even. Yet the story is intentionally included by Mark to say something about the inconvenience of God taking on a real body, with real flesh, real blood, and real spit. The Incarnation was not, in the first instance, a theological category with complicated philosophical resonances. It was an

5. Moltmann-Wendel, *I Am My Body*, xi.

event in the life of God, the becoming flesh with us and for us. The heart of that most intimate of spiritual encounters, the Eucharist, is nothing less than a celebration of Christ's lived yet broken body, given for broken, shamed, and rebellious humankind. It is surely significant, therefore, that the restoring and healing work of Christ is accomplished through the exposure of his own nakedness on the cross. When the soldiers threw dice to decide on who should be the owner of his clothing, Christ was above them in shameful, public, naked view. Somehow, as we shall see in due course, his own nakedness is a necessary component in redeeming and healing all those whose own bodies have been violated. "He himself bore our sins in his body on the cross, so that we might die to sins and live for righteousness; by his wounds you have been healed" (1 Pet 2:24).

We have now explored the contours and colors of shame from a variety of angles. We have seen how this cancer of the individual soul can so easily become an endemic disorder affecting a whole society. While it has significant political and social ramifications, it is at heart a spiritual crisis stemming from the disorientated direction that humankind faces in relation to God. We have also noted that because shame is both profoundly existential and deeply relational, it does not respond to legal solutions. Whatever healing and reconciliation is ushered into our world by the advent of Jesus Christ, it must be able to touch this sore in such a way that genuine transformation is effected. The mission of Jesus into a shame-filled world will form the substance of the second half of this book.

PART 2

Finding Honor

8

Judgment

THE RESTORATION, HEALING, AND reconciliation of the shamed, formed—
as we shall see in due course—a major focus of the mission of Jesus.
Shame is such a delicate, intimate, personal, and interpersonal issue that
it may at first sight seem strange to pair shame with the judgment of God.
Surely judgment is too strong and too blunt an instrument with which to
deal with the pervasive cancer that is shame. Yet shame is a multi-headed
hydra whose tentacles have enslaved and entangled humanity. Serious
surgery is needed to deal with the problem and it is at this place that the
searing judgment of God is so vitally necessary. At times shame is heaped
upon a person or a community from without. Such oppression needs to
be exposed for what it is. At other times shame is the natural bedfellow
of guilt, the inevitable consequence of actions that have fallen far short
of the glory and the love of God. That shame too needs to be brought out
from the shadows into the light. Sometimes shame has simply made its
unwanted presence felt in our lives, unconnected to any obvious failure,
not imposed intentionally from another, but simply there, brooding and
sapping the life of its host. Whatever the circumstances and origin, the
judgment of God is an entirely appropriate route by which shame can be
addressed.

The trouble is that "the judgment of God" is an emotionally laden
term. In the popular imagination, judgment suggests the fickle, vengeful, capricious rage of an impetuous deity bent on revenge. Indeed the

whole business of the crucifixion of Christ on the cross has, unfortunately, sometimes been represented in precisely this way. Some theological interpretations of the atonement have resorted to very judicial language in an attempt to depict the true nature of what was taking place on the cross where Jesus died. A legal "exchange" occurred, and upon the completion of this "exchange" two things, we are told, took place. The first is an alteration of our legal status before God. Without the crucifixion we all remain in a state of guilt before a holy God. We are in effect lawbreakers, transgressors, guilty criminals, and the cross removes this designation and replaces it with the word "innocent." The penalty for our lawbreaking has been paid, and we are allowed to leave the courtroom as innocent people. The transaction that has taken place has happened in some legal realm where the balancing of the books takes place. It is, therefore, an "objective" action that happens outside of us as it were. The second aspect of the exchange is that something happens within us, a subjective, deeply personal intervention within the private sphere. This intervention can be described as regeneration, the new birth, a new creation coming into being, an entirely altered orientation.

It is far from clear, however, whether the language of "exchange" is an adequate or even appropriate way in which to articulate what took place on Good Friday. Part of the problem is that exchange suggests some kind of reciprocal arrangement. An exchange takes place when we purchase a car, for example. We hand over the check and in return we are given the car. Yet is this how God functions, according to some kind of spiritual logic of equivalence? God places a demand for holiness and obedience upon humanity; this demand is not fulfilled, which inexorably leads to the demand for punishment, which in turn must be borne by someone. Jesus offers himself as the payment and the exchange mechanism comes full circle. The stories of Christ's involvement with the people that he encountered seem to tell a different story. John records the account of Jesus' first public foray in his ministry at the wedding at Cana. By placing this well-known story at the very beginning of his Gospel, John is signaling that this first miracle is a sign of things to come, bearing the hallmark or character of his entire ministry. The miracle at the wedding speaks loudly of the idea of "gift," and excessive gift at that. It is an example of the overabundance, the hyper-generosity of God. This quality is reaffirmed time and again in the gospels, perhaps most notably in the parable of the workers in the vineyard (Matt 20:1–16), in which the owner of the vineyard (God) is roundly criticized for being overly generous. It is the language of excess once more, the territory of gift, rather than the world of exchange. It is as if the revelatory work of Jesus was to expose fully the outrageous abundance of the gift of God, in opposition to the notion that God only operates on a strictly legal and equivalent basis.

The second problem with the judicial language of exchange is that it is not clear how the subjective repercussions of the atonement actually work. The announcement that a person is declared "innocent" in a legal sense does not necessarily or even automatically lead to a transformation inwardly. If God's primary intention is to maintain the legal ordering of the world, then the interpersonal, communal aspect of the work of Christ is relegated, at least potentially, to an optional extra. We are left with the image of God as cosmic law enforcer, an image closer to the ancient Greek pantheon of gods than the God revealed for us in Jesus Christ. Perhaps part of the problem is the tendency to associate law and justice too closely together. Laws are derived from the concept of justice and are usually culturally specific. Justice, on the other hand, has a more timeless quality about it and, in the hands of the biblical writers, has a distinctly restorative rather than punitive function and is always profoundly connected to the notion of covenant.

In tracing the outline of the story of God's reconciling love we are, from time to time, faced with the language of justice, in which God is depicted in the role of divine judge. We have already alluded to this term on several occasions, but it is now time to look at it more closely. For some, this form of language is highly problematic. It conjures up images of a cosmic tribunal in which God metes out justice and punishment to those whom he deems to be deserving of it. It forms part of a traditional image in which, on the Last Day, God will display his awesome capacity as the judge of all the earth and will come breathing fire and destruction on all those who are disobedient. It is essential, therefore, that we are careful how we define God's justice lest we too easily assume that the word, as used in the Bible, carries with it exactly the same meaning that is given to it today. Associated with the concept of "justice" are a cluster of words— wrath, judgment, and punishment—which, taken together, help us enter into a biblical mindset. Let us now turn to these terms in order to discern how, in the hands of the biblical writers, such language is used.

Wrath

We must be careful when reading the word "wrath" not to automatically ascribe to God a character trait that is merely a human projection, otherwise we end up with an image of God in which he feels great irritation and anger at the lifestyle of human beings and cannot help inflicting retributive punishment on them because of this great fury. The key question to ask therefore is this: How do the New Testament writers use this word?

We are introduced to the term quite early on with the explosive arrival of John the Baptist. John's vocation was simple. It was to extend his finger to point in one direction for the entire duration of his life. That finger pointed to the coming Christ, announcing his imminent arrival. Listen to him thunder in Matt 3:

> But when he saw many of the Pharisees and Sadducees coming to where he was baptizing, he said to them, "You brood of vipers! Who warned you to flee from the coming wrath? Produce fruit in keeping with repentance. And do not think you can say to yourselves, 'We have Abraham as our father.' I tell you that out of these stones God can raise up children for Abraham. The axe is already at the root of the trees, and every tree that does not produce good fruit will be cut down and thrown into the fire. I baptize you with water for repentance. But after me will come one who is more powerful than I, whose sandals I am not fit to carry. He will baptize you with the Holy Spirit and with fire. His winnowing fork is in his hand, and he will clear his threshing-floor, gathering his wheat into the barn and burning up the chaff with unquenchable fire." (Matt 3:7–10)

The shocking thing to notice in Matthew's account of John the Baptist's ministry is that when he addresses the Pharisees and the Sadducees, he describes the arrival of Jesus Christ on earth as "the coming wrath." For John—and therefore, by implication, for us—wrath is not an abstraction connected with another abstract concept, namely justice; rather wrath is intimately connected with a person—Jesus, the Savior of the world. Typically the Incarnation is nowadays depicted in somewhat romantic terms, associated with the helpless infant born in a manger in all his acute vulnerability, the victim of persecution and rejection. Yet for John, the coming of Christ into the world is synonymous with wrath, especially directed at the religious leaders of his day. What content can we therefore give to this word "wrath" when it has to be defined specifically with reference to Jesus?

The immediate context gives us a clue. This Jesus, to whom John constantly points, possesses a winnowing fork. The task of a winnower is to separate the grain from the chaff, a task that, according to John, Jesus came to perform. The ability to separate or discern, to know the difference between good and evil, is an ability that only God possesses. Left to ourselves we, as fallible humans, are unable to truly know the difference between light and dark, good and bad, healthy and poisoned. For us there are so many shades of grey, so many undefined possibilities, so many mitigating circumstances and subordinate moral clauses, that we are often simply at a loss to know how to make a judgment. This is why Jesus warns against judging others, most notably in his Sermon on the Mount. Yet a time will come, Jesus often reiterates, when God will reveal and make apparent what appears to us to be so muddied. "There is nothing concealed that will not be disclosed, or hidden that will not be made known," says Jesus in Matt 10:27.

John the Baptist's fierce denunciation of the Pharisees and Sadducees in his riverside congregation, warning them of the wrath to come, invites us to explore those occasions when that wrath of Christ was most evident. Matthew 23 is particularly instructive here, for we witness the wrath of Jesus being poured out in withering speech upon the teachers of the law and the Pharisees. The seven woes articulated there deal with the variety of manifestations of oppression—under the guise of religious observance—that these groups were displaying. These Pharisees love the place of honor, they tie up heavy loads and put them on men's shoulders, they shut the kingdom of heaven in men's faces and they have neglected the more important matters of the law—justice, mercy and faithfulness. Taken as a whole this devastating indictment speaks of oppression, making captive and excluding all those who did not belong to their inner circle. It is for such people alone, at least in Matthew's account, that Jesus reserves his wrath. In speaking in this way he was using his winnowing fork to expose their oppressive practices and hypocrisy. His wrath, however, betrayed his deep compassion for those who had suffered at their hands. Who were those excluded, exploited people? They were the shamed, the people whose value and dignity had been ripped away. The wrath of God must be located, therefore, within the loving heart of God and be seen as an expression of the ferocity of that love. Any parent who stands idle while witnessing abuse and violence being heaped upon their own child, does not display love. To exhibit wrath at such moments is an entirely appropriate expression of the intensity of love that a parent has for a child. God's wrath is his passionate desire for his own creation.

In addition to the aspect of wrath that is concerned with exposure, there is a further shade of meaning, which we find articulated by Paul in his letter to the Romans. Here Paul describes God's wrath not as active punishment but rather in terms of a "giving over." "The wrath of God is being revealed from heaven against all the godlessness and wickedness of men who suppress the truth by their wickedness . . . therefore God *gave them over* in the sinful desires of their hearts," writes Paul in Rom 1:24. It is as if Paul is saying that God chooses to let wayward human beings face the consequences of their actions. He does not stop them but lets them go. This "giving over" is far from being the soft option. It is God allowing us to face the inevitable, terrible consequences of living without boundaries, without restraint, and without him. This is a more passive depiction of God's wrath but in reality no less awesome. It is an image that is drawn not from a legal environment where there is a kind of heavenly tribunal but from the family. Any family with adolescent children will know of the struggles to achieve that delicate balance between freedom and restraint. Sometimes there are determined young people who insist on going their own way and the reluctant decision of loving parents is to "let them go," acutely aware of the pain and anxiety that arise from this choice. The act of letting go is not an action that speaks of rejection, but the exact opposite. It is the unconditional love that parents have for their offspring that enables them to make this agonized decision. God's action in giving people over needs to be understood within the context of a family metaphor thereby ensuring that his wrath remains consistent with his love. To locate the concept of wrath solely within a legal metaphor risks losing this loving nuance. What we end up with is an image of God that is primarily concerned with retributive justice. That is the face we see first, yet behind this angry visage there is really a loving, compassionate God after all. But sadly God's grace is hidden for many behind images of his anger, his burning wrath. This is surely a dangerous distortion. God desires to be known as *slow to anger and filled with compassion*. His very essence is love. Everything he does is an expression of his love. Even his wrath—his handing over—is done with tears in his eyes, as it were, as he lets us go our own stubborn ways. He is a God who longs, yearns, and aches for the lost and the captive. His wrath is directed against those who oppress, imprison, and abuse.

Justice

In addition to wrath we need to explore the meaning of the New Testament concept of "judging." The most commonly used word for the judging process is *krino*; and its meaning is perhaps best explicated in Matt 13:24–30, in the parable of the wheat and the tares.

> Jesus told them another parable: "The kingdom of heaven is like a man who sowed good seed in his field. But while everyone was sleeping, his enemy came and sowed weeds among the wheat, and went away. When the wheat sprouted and formed ears, then the weeds also appeared. The owner's servants came to him and said, 'Sir, didn't you sow good seed in your field? Where then did the weeds come from?' 'An enemy did this,' he replied. The servants asked him, 'Do you want us to go and pull them up?' 'No,' he answered, 'because while you are pulling the weeds, you may root up the wheat with them. Let both grow together until the harvest. At that time I will tell the harvesters: First collect the weeds and tie them in bundles to be burned; then gather the wheat and bring it into my barn.'"

Here Jesus warns his disciples that they are not to pass premature judgment on one another. One simply cannot discern between wheat and tares with sufficient precision, so it is best not to attempt to do so at all. One day God himself will make that judgment; he will judge by making clear, separating, defining, and exposing. When God judges it is with the intention of revealing what is. This is the primary import of *krino*. The intention of such judgment is not to impose a penalty but rather to expose, to reveal, and to make obvious to all. It is precisely because it is only God who is able to rightly discern the difference between good and evil that this capability is his prerogative alone. Perhaps that is the reason for the prohibition given to Adam and Eve in the garden. The desire to know the difference between good and evil betrayed a desire to be equal with God.

New Testament language builds upon the ancient Hebrew tradition of covenantal justice. Jewish justice was not based on an abstract notion, but was intensely earthy, concerned with the messiness of human life. In Jewish culture, justice was not dispensed according to absolute, detached, moral standards but rather sought to restore peace and harmony within a community. To live in a healthy, open, trusting relationship with one's neighbor was to be in a "just" relationship. The intention of the maintenance of justice was always *relational*—concerned with reconciliation—rather than legal, which is more focused on retribution. It is most likely that the pressing question in the culture of the Old Testament would have been, "How can this person, who has caused a disruption to the harmonious functioning of our community, be re-instated and included once more in such a way as to ensure that they are not 'shamed,' but their misdemeanor has nevertheless been taken seriously?"

Two important Hebrew words accompanying this concept are often found side by side. One is *tsĕdāqâ* and the other is *mišpāt*. The former carries the meaning of the one who establishes a framework, a covenant, within which one may live in peace and shalom. The latter refers to the one who maintains equity, particularly for the downtrodden and defenseless. This pair of words often go together, as in Ps 99:4: "The King is mighty, he loves justice [*mišpāt*]—you have established equity; in Jacob you have done what is just [*mišpāt*] and right [*tsĕdāqâ*]." When a king demonstrated social justice for the widows, the poor, the strangers, and the shamed, then he was deemed to be fulfilling the expectations of *mišpāt* and *tsĕdāqâ*. In fact, when an earthly ruler behaved in this manner he was mirroring the activity of God himself. The prophet Amos called out in this very language, claiming that one day God will come to judge the oppressors and the oppressed alike. Amos speaks as if he is uttering God's own thoughts: "I hate, I despise your religious feasts; I cannot stand your assemblies. Even though you bring me burnt offerings and grain offerings, I will not accept them. Though you bring choice fellowship offerings, I will have no regard for them. Away with the noise of your songs! I will not listen to the music of your harps. But let justice [*mišpāt*] roll on like a river, righteousness [*tsĕdāqâ*] like a never-failing stream!"

This call for God to act justly is echoed repeatedly in the prophetic writings. The pinnacle of all that is demanded of humankind is simply to mimic the actions of God. Hear the words of the prophet Micah: "He has showed you, O man, what is good. And what does the LORD require of you? To act justly [*mišpāt*] and to love mercy and to walk humbly with your God." Whenever *mišpāt* and *tsĕdāqâ* are found the inevitable result is the demonstration of mercy, as this verse so eloquently demonstrates. The prayer of King Solomon, recorded for us in Ps 72, reveals this too. He asked for the ability to rule his people with the justice of God. "Endow the king with your justice, O God, the royal son with your righteousness. He will judge your people in righteousness, your afflicted ones with justice." When Solomon possessed God's judicial ability, then he would be able to restore equity, mercy, protection, and provision to all the people who lived in the land.

If the ancient Hebrew concept of justice had such a strong relational element to it, it is not surprising that we find biblical instances of corporate justice-making. In a village context all the citizens had the right to voice an opinion on a matter of justice. This can be observed, for example, at the conclusion of the story of Ruth, the foreign woman from neighboring Moab who had found herself in Israel as an economic migrant. Once her ancestry had become evident the village convened a meeting to decide on how she should be cared for. It is an example of Old Testament "justice."

> Meanwhile Boaz went up to the town gate and sat there. When the kinsman-redeemer he had mentioned came along, Boaz said, "Come over here, my friend, and sit down." So he went over and sat down.
>
> Boaz took ten of the elders of the town and said, "Sit here," and they did so. Then he said to the kinsman-redeemer, "Naomi, who has come back from Moab, is selling the piece of land that belonged to our brother Elimelech. I thought I should bring the matter to your attention and suggest that you buy it in the presence of these seated here and in the presence of the elders of my people. If you will redeem it, do so. But if you will not, tell me, so I will know. For no one has the right to do it except you, and I am next in line."
>
> "I will redeem it," he said.
>
> Then Boaz said, "On the day you buy the land from Naomi and from Ruth the Moabitess, you acquire the dead man's widow, in order to maintain the name of the dead with his property."
>
> At this, the kinsman-redeemer said, "Then I cannot redeem it because I might endanger my own estate. You redeem it yourself. I cannot do it."
>
> (Now in earlier times in Israel, for the redemption and transfer of property to become final, one party took off his sandal and

gave it to the other. This was the method of legalizing transactions in Israel.)

So the kinsman-redeemer said to Boaz, "Buy it yourself." And he removed his sandal.

Then Boaz announced to the elders and all the people, "Today you are witnesses that I have bought from Naomi all the property of Elimelech, Kilion and Mahlon. I have also acquired Ruth the Moabitess, Mahlon's widow, as my wife, in order to maintain the name of the dead with his property, so that his name will not disappear from among his family or from the town records. Today you are witnesses!"

Then the elders and all those at the gate said, "We are witnesses. May the LORD make the woman who is coming into your home like Rachel and Leah, who together built up the house of Israel. May you have standing in Ephrathah and be famous in Bethlehem. Through the offspring the LORD gives you by this young woman, may your family be like that of Perez, whom Tamar bore to Judah.

(Ruth 4:1–12)

The concern of the village elders centered around how they were to preserve the honor of the name of Elimelech, the deceased husband of Naomi. Boaz, out of love for both Naomi and Ruth, offers to buy his estate and in so doing take on the responsibility of caring for these two women. Ruth could now marry Boaz, and their offspring would perpetuate the family name thereby avoiding the threat of shame. Thus the purpose of dispensing justice in this case was to include, to restore, and to protect. It was, above all, a covenantal, relational form of justice. By acting in this way the people were doing nothing less than reflecting in their communal life together the way in which God provides justice. Listen to the words of Deut 10:17–18: "For the LORD your God is God of gods and Lord of lords, the great God, mighty and awesome, who shows no partiality and accepts no bribes. He defends the cause of the fatherless and the widow, and loves the alien, giving him food and clothing."

The apostle Paul's usage of the term "wrath" flows from his own immersion in these Hebrew Scriptures. So when he writes, for example, in Rom 12:19, "do not take revenge, my friends, but leave room for God's wrath, for it is written, 'It is mine to avenge, I will repay,' says the Lord,'" the words should be understood against the background of the Jewish Scriptures. However, to the contemporary Western reader they carry the connotation of divine violence. This is precisely where the difficulty with the language of cosmic, legal, retributive justice lies. If the world is already characterized by human aggression, does this mean that God also operates in this way, fighting violence with violence and entering into an economy of legal exchange? Yet, on closer examination, in the context of Paul's whole argument, he is urging his readers to learn how to love their enemies. They are to feed those who oppose them, give them water to drink and care for their needs. In the midst of the flow of his writing he quotes from Deut 32:35, "It is mine to avenge; I will repay." This passage goes on to speak in the following verse about God's vindication of those who are oppressed. "The LORD will judge his people and have compassion on his servants when he sees their strength is gone and no one is left, slave or free." So it is possible to read this text not in terms of God's desire to be drawn into the circle of violence that mars our world, but in terms of "God's hyper-judicial concern for the victimized other," as the theologian Kevin Vanhoozer expresses it.[1] In other words, the texts that appear to support the view that God's wrath and judgment are vengeful and punitive in reality belong to the language of God's loving, unconditional covenant with his people. His wrath is the exposure of the oppressive practices that enslave and diminish others. Such a "wrath" emerges from the intensity of his love that cannot bear to see his creation distorted and destroyed.

Closely connected to the concept of judgment is the distinctly Pauline term "justify," derived from the Greek word (*dikaios*). Paul uses this term repeatedly, and the words "righteous," "righteousness," and "justification" are all derived from this root. The theme of justification has been the scene of many a theological battle over the centuries and was the turf upon which Luther stood his ground when he nailed his ninety-five theses to the door of Wittenberg Castle Church in 1517. This is not the place to rehearse the various strands of theological contention on the matter, but if we look more closely at one particular text in the flow of Paul's argument in his Letter to the Romans, namely Rom 3:22–24, then further light might be shed on how he uses this word. The sentence in question is: "There is no difference between Jew and Gentile, for all have sinned and fall short of the glory of God, and all are justified freely by his grace through the redemption that came by Christ Jesus." Paul is addressing a mixed group of congregations in the city of Rome at a time when com-

---

1. Vanhoozer, "The Atonement in Postmodernity," 378.

petition for honor was fierce. His letter forcefully asserts that there are, in reality, absolutely no grounds upon which any group can claim superior status in comparison with anyone else, because there is "no difference" between Jew or Gentile, for everyone falls short. The phrase "to fall short" is itself referring to the acquisition of honor, which means that when Paul adopts this phrase he is in fact saying "that all fall short of the transcendent standard of honor."[2] No nation or cultural grouping possesses a more honorable status than another, yet, despite this, something momentous has happened through the advent of Jesus Christ. That something is the free gift of grace, which means that all are in the process of being set right (*dikaioumenoi*, a verb used in the passive voice). The sense of the phrase is not to be understood in some kind of forensic way, addressing a legal problem. Paul was steeped in Hebrew thinking in which everything is framed within covenantal, relational terms. To be "set right" is to be in a right relationship with oneself, with the wider community, and with God. It is to be given an honor that is entirely independent of any national heritage or performance. To be put right is to be included freely in the community that is the people of God. N. T. Wright has expressed the sense of Paul's "justification" terminology in this way: "In standard Christian theological language, it wasn't so much about soteriology as about ecclesiology; not so much about salvation as about the church."[3] Whilst the language of justification belongs to the legal realm, the term is used in an entirely non-legal manner. To declare that someone is "forgiven" is to acknowledge that a misdeed has been committed which is now absolved. Forgiveness addresses the act of commission or omission in relation to a standard, but does nothing to address the deeper malaise of shame. To be declared "justified," however, is of an entirely different order. It is to declare a complete and total acceptance of someone by an act of compassionate grace. It is to be put on a right relationship once more. This is how David Rhoades expresses the difference: "When you say, 'you are forgiven' you are dealing with the act, but not always with the shame that underlies the act. When you say 'you are accepted' . . . you address not only the sin but also the underlying shame for being the kind of person that would

---

2. Jewett, *Romans*, 280.

3. Wright, *What St. Paul Really Said*, 119.

commit such a sin/crime. And you liberate the person from the tyranny of the system that caused the shame."[4]

Punishment

In addition to the terms "wrath," "judgment," and "justify," one other term belonging to the cluster of words surrounding the concept of justice is "punishment." Some theories of the atonement insist that God not only actively does punish but *has* to punish because of the demands of justice. There are only a few verses in the New Testament where the term punishment is used in association with the judgment of God. One of these is Matt 25:46, "And these shall go away into everlasting punishment but the righteous into life eternal." This sentence comes at the conclusion of a challenging address by Jesus in which he depicts the way in which the judgment of God will one day be manifested. God's concern for the needy is vividly highlighted and he points out the failure of those who have been unaware of the desperate social conditions all around them. Christ's utter identification with the poor and the forgotten is made crystal clear when he says: "For I was hungry and you gave me nothing to eat, I was thirsty and you gave me nothing to drink, I was a stranger and you did not invite me in, I needed clothes and you did not clothe me, I was sick and in prison and you did not look after me" (Matt 25:42–43). The word translated as "punishment" in verse 46 is *kolasis* and is derived from the Greek word—*kolos*—for a dwarf, and thus carries the sense of "to make smaller" or "to curtail" or "to prune." This is how the New Testament commentator William Barclay writes about this particular verse.

> One of the key passages is Matt 25:46 where it is said that the rejected go away to eternal punishment, and the righteous to eternal life. The Greek word for punishment is *kolasis*, which was not originally an ethical word at all. It originally meant the pruning of trees to make them grow better. I think it is true to say that in all Greek secular literature *kolasis* is never used of anything but remedial punishment. The word for "eternal" is *aionios*. It means more than "everlasting," for Plato—who may have invented the word—plainly says that a thing may be everlasting and still not be *aionios*. The simplest way out is that *aionios* cannot be used properly of anyone but God; it is the word uniquely, as Plato saw it,

4. Rhoades, "Justification by Grace," 89.

> [applicable to] God. Eternal punishment is then literally that kind of remedial punishment which it befits God to give and which only God can give.[5]

This suggests that the punishment described is one that involves a disciplinary restoration of the person. Those who endure this punishment are those who have not fed the hungry or visited the imprisoned. God's punishment is for those who have consistently failed to notice those who remain on the margins of society—the hungry, the destitute, and those in prison. The verse illustrates once more God's passionate concern for the shamed.

The second text in which punishment is mentioned is Heb 10:29 and it illustrates the use of the Greek word *timorias*. "How much more severely do you think someone deserves to be punished [*timorias*] who has trampled the Son of God underfoot, who has treated as an unholy thing the blood of the covenant that sanctified them, and who has insulted the Spirit of grace?" The word here translated as punishment (*timorias*) is used only once in the entire New Testament. It is derived from the word *timē* meaning "to pay a price," or in other words to face the consequences of an action or previously made choice. The writer of the book of Hebrews is dealing with a pastoral situation and is writing to Christians, not to those who make no claim to any kind of allegiance to the Christian faith. His concern is that their lives should be marked by "love and good deeds" (Heb 10:24). It is the lifestyle of these professing Christians that is in focus, and not the fate of those who have never heard of Christ or who have not yet "received the truth" (Heb 10:26). When these professing Christians live lives that are characterized by the same greed, arrogance, and pride as the pervading culture, then they effectively "trample" on the name of Christ and publicly bring that name into disrepute. One day that profound hypocrisy will be exposed for what it is and they will face the consequences of their actions. Those actions will be revealed and their shame will thus become evident.

Two further Greek words however deserve consideration in this context. One is *paideias* and is translated as "punish" in the NIV and "chastening" in the KJV (Heb 12:6). Here is the NIV rendering of Heb 12:6: "because the Lord disciplines those he loves, and he punishes everyone he accepts as a son." The meaning of the word is provided by the context

5. http://www.auburn.edu/%7Eallenkc/barclay1.html.

of the discussion. The writer is referring to God's discipline and training of his people. He likens this to the way in which a father would discipline and train his own children. In fact, he *only* does this to his own children, not to everyone. It is precisely because they are his children that he exercises *paideias* over them. There is no sense in which this word is used here as expressing the doctrine that God "punishes" those who are not (yet) his children.

The final word in the cluster of punishment terms is *dike*, which is found only three times in the New Testament. One of these occasions is found in Paul's Second Letter to the Thessalonians. It is a pastoral epistle written to encourage small, persecuted Christian communities in Asia Minor. The public disgrace, humiliation, and suffering that they were enduring was a great trial to them and constituted significant loss. Paul writes to inform them that such aggressors would one day face a penal judgment[6] and the use of the word *dike* indicates that this was precisely his intention. There is clearly a place in Paul's thinking, therefore, for some kind of penal sanction against aggressors and those who diminish the value and dignity of human life. Such punishment would ruin their previous status and reputation and expose them to the searing judgment of God. For those who have been the innocent victims of crimes committed against them to be assured that in God's economy a due and fitting punishment will be levied against the perpetrators would be a source of solace and empowerment.

No discussion of the role of "punishment" with reference to the death of Christ would be complete without reference to the text in Isa 53:5, which is often translated in this way: "But he was pierced for our transgressions, he was crushed for our iniquities; the punishment that brought us peace was upon him, and by his wounds we are healed." At first sight this text does indeed point prophetically towards the coming of Christ who would take upon himself the wrath and punishment of God the Father. For many people today this is a disturbing text. The key word for the purposes of our discussion here is the Hebrew word *mûsar*, a noun that means a "rebuke" or some form of corrective discipline. It is not a punitive word but one that suggests correction with the intent of bringing

---

6. "He will punish those who do not know God and do not obey the gospel of our Lord Jesus. They will be punished with everlasting destruction and shut out from the presence of the Lord and from the glory of his might" (2 Thess 1:8–9).

back into line. It has associations with a bit and bridle that one might place on a horse in order to ride it. With this in mind the Isaiah text sounds as if the prophet is declaring that one day the "Servant of the Lord" would bring a wayward world back into a true and healthy alignment with God the Creator. Understood this way the text offers an alternative picture of the healing love of God.

How does this discussion of the justice of God and the move away from the language of exchange towards the language of gift and excess address the question of shame? If shame is the central "problem" needing to be addressed, then it becomes immediately obvious the legal language is rendered inappropriate. Anyone who has felt the shocking, traumatizing experience of shame will know that punitive and retributive language does nothing to heal or to transform. The restorative justice of God and the alienation of shame need to be brought into contact with one another, to find a touching point.

We shall conclude this chapter with an example from rural Nigeria to shed some light on this possibility. When my wife and I lived there in the early 1980s we were told that in a traditional, pre-modern Nigerian village justice was administered collectively. If a member of the village committed a crime—the stealing of sheep, for example—and his misdemeanor became evident, then the whole village felt the shame of this transgression. The harmony of the village had been violated and the perpetrator needed to be dealt with. In such cases the normal procedure was that the villagers would come together to dance and in so doing would sing a song about the stolen sheep. The dancing would continue for several hours, thereby exposing to public view the crime that had been committed. One can easily image the humiliation that the thief would have felt. The purpose of the dancing and singing was twofold. The first was to expose and the second was to restore back into fellowship. It was not punitive in the sense of demanding retribution, but it was nevertheless a highly effective form of justice in which reconciliation lay at the heart. Could it be that God's justice is similar to this, both exposing and reconciling the shamed simultaneously? The healing occurs in the context of belonging to a community in which full acceptance is found.

9

Sacrifice and Grace

OUR INITIAL EXAMINATION OF the story of Adam and Eve's expulsion from the garden hinted at the possibility that despite the loss of intimacy with their Creator, God would nevertheless demonstrate mercy in the midst of judgment. An animal was "sacrificed" to make them warm clothes, and God, the tailor, undertook the task himself. In tracing the story of Israel, which is part of the bigger story of Christ, it is appropriate that we pause to examine one central feature of the life of God's chosen people, namely the issue of sacrifice. To the ears of contemporary listeners, the whole notion of sacrifice is troublesome. It conjures up images of gruesome immolations on sacrificial altars with a disturbing emphasis on blood and the death of a victim. It suggests that a temperamental deity can only be placated through violent means. In what way is such an ancient and apparently primitive practice at all helpful in addressing our human condition? And how does sacrifice actually change anything? To address these questions we need to return to the biblical narrative to observe what part sacrificial rituals played in the life of God's chosen people.

The Meaning of "Sacrifice"

As they journeyed through the desert en route to the promised land the Israelites were given detailed instructions covering all aspects of civil and religious life. A large part of our struggle to understand these regulations is that our cultural milieu in the twenty-first century makes a sharp distinction between church ordinance and civil governance. The two realms are kept legally distinct with entirely different jurisdictions. To the Hebrew mind such distinctions would have been puzzling at best. For them, the whole of life was to be lived within the gracious care of the God who had delivered them from slavery such that the demarcation between civil life and worship was blurred. At the heart of their lifestyle lay the obligation to bring sacrifices to Yahweh. There were distinct times and seasons in which these sacrificial offerings were to be brought to the priests, such that the yearly calendar was peppered with occasions to express gratitude, thanksgiving, repentance, peace, and forgiveness. The sacrificial system provided the framework through which such human needs could be addressed.

Considerable scholarly energy has been expended on the meaning of these practices and how they effected forgiveness or atonement. One strand of interpretation contends that it is through the shedding of blood that a change occurs within God and he is enabled to grant forgiveness to the supplicant. In order for God to forgive, a blood sacrifice needs to be offered. It is via the means of the death of a substitute that forgiveness is granted. The primary theological objection to this is that such an interpretation constrains the actions of God. He "needs," or even "requires," a blood sacrifice and without such he is simply unable to offer forgiveness. Clearly to restrict God's freedom in this way makes little sense. God is always free, always acts in love, and exists under no external pressure impinging upon his intervention in his creation.[1] So, theoretically at least, God does not "need" or "require" sacrifice. He could simply say a word and we would be healed.

An alternative reading is that it is not in God that the change occurs but in the one offering the sacrifice, who is "made clean" or "purged" of guilt. Somehow, mysteriously, a purging of the soul occurs at the moment of offering and the worshipper is declared "forgiven" and "clean." Using the language of the law court, the one accused is now declared innocent and the prosecution has no further claim on the life of the person in the dock. The limitations of this view of sacrifice are manifold too. The perennial intention of God is to restore relationship, to reconcile to himself the whole of creation. For this to happen there needs to be *a change of heart*; in fact,

---

1. See later for my response to the correct insight that "justice is not a principle external to God but part of his nature."

an entirely altered orientation. Some profound change needs to take place within us, not simply above us, in some higher legal realm where justice is administered and sentences passed. To simply declare that someone may go free does nothing to ensure that any internal change has been effected; there is merely a different legal relationship. If the offering of sacrifice has some kind of automatic transforming effect upon the worshipper, it is by no means clear what this is. The danger with some interpretations of sacrifice in the Old Testament is that one ends up with a quasi-magical if not mechanical view. Once the sacrifice has been presented this automatically triggers either a response in God or a change in the person.

It is my view that neither of these interpretations effectively addresses the question of how the slaughter of an animal or the presentation of part of a harvest has any real effect on anything. A mechanistic approach to sacrifice was roundly condemned by the prophet Micah, who thundered

> With what shall I come before the LORD and bow down before the exalted God? Shall I come before him with burnt offerings, with calves a year old? Will the LORD be pleased with thousands of rams, with ten thousand rivers of oil? Shall I offer my firstborn for my transgression, the fruit of my body for the sin of my soul? He has showed you, O man, what is good. And what does the LORD require of you? To act justly and to love mercy and to walk humbly with your God. (Mic 6:6–8)

Micah protested that the people had misunderstood the whole purpose of sacrifice, making the ritual into some kind of spiritual mathematical equation in which the more animals that were killed the greater the forgiveness offered by God in return. What then is the key to understanding the meaning of sacrifice? It is contained in Lev 17:11, where we read, "For the life of a creature is in the blood, and I have given it to you to make atonement for yourselves on the altar; it is the blood that makes atonement for one's life." Here the text asserts that the blood is a symbol of *life*, not of death. When the worshipper presented his best lamb for a sacrifice, the lamb at that point became a representative of the whole person. *In the shedding of the blood of the lamb, the worshipper was symbolically offering his entire life to God, in a costly manner.* This offering was indicative of the state of his heart. By giving away that which was dear to him, whether it was a bull, a lamb, a pigeon, or some wheat, the worshipper was taking the radical step of trusting that Yahweh would provide for his family even though something precious had just been given away. The riskiness of this step is easy to miss. Here was a nomadic peasant community, dependent on their flocks for sustenance, and they are challenged to offer from their estate that which is perfect, without blemish, and therefore of greatest value. Doing so would, from a human point of view, place their family in increased jeopardy. If they gave away that which was most valuable, they were placing their family at greater risk. To offer a sacrifice was to symbolically offer one's life in trusting dependence on Yahweh in reorientation once more.

Did this action bring about an automatic ontological change in the worshipper? Or did this ritual performance in itself produce "cleansing"? The texts give no indication that this took place. Did, however, the action have an effect on the worshipper? I would surmise that the effect was profound. By taking such a risky step and by symbolically turning to face Yahweh, the worshipper would undoubtedly have been touched in a deep manner. Did the action of offering a sacrifice produce a corresponding reaction in God? Did it, in effect, "enable" God to forgive? Phrased in this way, the question is somewhat absurd. There is nothing that compels God's hand, nothing that compromises his utter freedom. God is not liberated to forgive as a result of witnessing the shedding of blood. What then is the point of the sacrifice and how does it effect any substantive change? To answer this one must place the question within a much broader framework concerned with how any change is brought into effect through the action of God. And here we are driven back once more to the story of creation in Gen 1.

The story begins with the repeated refrain—"and God said . . ." It was through the spoken word of God that the cosmos came into being. God's words are *speech acts*—when God speaks, something actually occurs, an event takes place. Let's consider an ordinary human example of this phenomenon. When, for instance, a couple say the words "I do," in the context of a marriage service, the resultant effect is quite different from the occasion when one might say "I do" in answer to the question, "do you like vanilla ice cream?" In a marriage service, uttering those two small words is enough to bring about a completely altered relationship between two people. It is *speech that is also action*, and this is how the speech of God functions. When God speaks, something changes, or is brought into being. It is the word of God that brings life or death, it the voice of God that declares forgiveness, it is the loud shout of Christ that raises Lazarus from the dead. So the answer to the question, "Does the offering of a blood sacrifice automatically elicit a response of forgiveness from God?" must surely be a resounding no! Does God declare by his spoken word that we are forgiven, set free, liberated, and made whole in his free response to a risky, daring act of trust? Then the answer must surely be yes! Framed in this way the whole question of blood sacrifice ceases to be the gruesome spectacle of a bloodthirsty deity who will only be placated with death, but rather the symbolic turning of the worshipper in love and trust towards God and the offering of his or her whole life to the God who only has to say a word and we are healed.

Anselm and Satisfaction

This interpretation of the tradition of sacrifice has significant implications for our understanding of the crucifixion. One strand of Christian theology has, over the centuries, interpreted the sacrifice of Christ on the cross in terms of "satisfying" the judicial demands of a holy God. It was a theology developed over the centuries by Cyprian, Tertullian, and perhaps most fully in the Middle Ages by Anselm. In the centuries prior to Anselm, theological attempts to interpret the atonement had given a significant dramatic role to Satan as one of the key players in a cosmic drama. The commonly held view was that humanity had fallen captive to Satan and that God, through the work of Christ, effected a way of releasing the captives from Satan's grip. A deal was struck, therefore, by which God would offer Christ as a ransom payment to Satan in return for the liberation of humankind. This kind of theological construction adopted the New Testament language of "ransom" yet, in Anselm's view, pushed that metaphor too far, using it to explain more than it was capable of explaining.

Anselm sought to rectify this distortion and moved away from the language of ransom, drawing instead on the language of the law court. This kind of legal thinking had already been proposed by Tertullian and Augustine in earlier centuries, and it is pertinent to note that both of these early thinkers had legal backgrounds. Anselm lived at a time when society was ordered on a feudal basis. The majority of the land was owned by a few wealthy landlords who allowed their peasants to live on the land. Within a feudal order there was a complex arrangement of both rights and obligations. The feudal Lord had the right to levy taxes; the peasants were under obligation to satisfy the demands of their Lord and, in return, they were permitted to remain on the land and enjoy a measure of security. If it worked well, it provided a basis for a peaceful and orderly society. Anselm believed that God worked in a similar way to this. We are the tenants on his land, with obligations towards God, whose task is to uphold order. Anselm's concern was to develop a theology that would explain how God maintained this order in the world without everything degenerating into chaos. In the absence of order there could be no harmony and God's honor could not be perceived.

What then should happen if there is a breach or disruption in this orderly world? If God, like a feudal landlord, is offended, then the safe ordering of the world is threatened. God must act, not because he is personally affronted, but because the order and beauty of the universe is at stake. Any offense against the authority of God was, in the opinion of Anselm, extremely serious. If the divine obligations have not been met then justice demands that satisfaction must, somehow, be made. Yet humanity in all its frailty simply cannot make adequate satisfaction. God is faced, therefore, with a dilemma. Either he must impose punishment for the failure to meet the required obligations, or satisfaction from another source must be found. Whilst Anselm did couch his arguments within a legal framework, his concern was not primarily to do with satisfying an abstract principle of justice. Rather, he was intent on demonstrating the way in which a distorted or even severed relationship between God and humanity could be satisfactorily restored. It was left to later theologians to take Anselm's thought and push it further and further in a legal direction, such that the notion of God as a personally affronted divine judge took far greater prominence. Colin Gunton has commented on this development in his book *The Actuality of the Atonement*. He writes, "Without doubt, many Western theologies of atonement have tended to be legalistic, making it appear that God is a God of law before he is a God of love, rather than the reverse, and so failing to do justice to the personal, relational, aspects of the matter."[2]

There are, however, a number of dimensions to the concept of satisfaction that are troublesome. The first is that the notion of satisfaction, as deployed in many popular sermons, presumes upon an ideal of jus-

2. Gunton, *The Actuality of the Atonement*, 87.

tice that must at all times be adhered to. It is as if God would love to simply forgive us, to say that all our sins are remembered no more, they are wiped away, but he *cannot* do that, much as he would like to. The reason being that there is something higher than God, namely justice, to which even God must bow. God is constrained in his actions by the demands of justice, which are immovable. We are on dangerous ground here if we assert, however implicitly, that there is another "god" behind God. Behind the loving face of the Father sits another, higher god, whose name is Justice. And Justice must always be obeyed, even by God himself. Clearly such a notion makes no sense and we must be careful to avoid such a way of thinking. Furthermore, there are a number of occasions in the New Testament when Jesus deliberately appears to depict God as *failing* to fulfill the demands of justice. Witness, for example, the parable of the prodigal son where the elder brother is aggrieved at the (apparently) unfairly generous treatment of his wayward brother. Or the parable of the workers in the vineyard where the vineyard owner unfairly pays everyone the same. In both of these instances God is portrayed as being unfairly generous, unjustly exuberant. This surely does not fit with the notion of a God who has to obey the demands of justice ("justice" here understood as the retributive balancing of divine rewards and punishments with human deeds).

However, justice, as a metaphor for the action of God, is an entirely valid and important term within a biblical framework. It needs to be carefully interpreted, however, otherwise we are in danger of importing meanings derived from our own cultural environment, with scant regard for the way in which the biblical writers understood the term. Justice is inextricably linked to the notion of law and in both the Old and New Testaments there is no interest in law in *abstract* terms. Laws were given and administered only within the context of a covenantal relationship, the bond between God and his people. The function of law was tied intimately to the maintenance of the integrity of the life of the community. As such it was thoroughly relational, personal, and corporate in its outworking. Once this covenantal mooring is loosened, the door is open for more legal, impersonal, and moralistic conceptions of justice to emerge. This is precisely what happened to theology in the hands of the early Latin theologians who displayed an impulse to drive theology away from the relational towards the legal. In this world, God becomes the one whose task it is to make demands upon humankind. The obligation placed upon us is therefore to satisfy those demands and thereby to fulfill certain divine obligations. The action of God is reduced thereby to an exercise of power, rather than a display of love.

The second area that is problematic is that the popular Christian notion of having to "satisfy" God in some way implies that God needs to be satisfied, that God is needy and therefore lacking something vital. If we claim that God *requires* or *demands* satisfaction we are depicting a God who is *not self-sufficient* or self-contained; that his being is incomplete and can only be fulfilled by the death of Christ on the cross. To even suggest a lack within God in this way surely elicits a response of "How absurd!" God does not lack anything and his freedom is thus never constrained or impinged upon. A god who requires satisfaction has the hallmarks of the Greek or Roman pantheon of deities who were constantly needing to be placated. Now clearly anyone who thinks of satisfaction in such ways is mistaken.

However, it may still be possible to imagine ways in which traditional Christian theology can speak of God's *requirement* of justice that do not fall into such popular errors. For traditional theology in its more sophisticated forms, as opposed to some of its more popular presentations, justice is not to be thought of as an external "god" sitting secretly "behind" the loving face of God, demanding to be fulfilled. Rather justice is one of God's qualities—part of his nature—alongside his love and his patience, and therefore when God judges he does so in accordance with his own character. Nothing outside of God is forcing him to judge. He does so because he is a just God. This is undoubtedly correct and a vast improvement on the popular misunderstandings of which we have spoken so far. Nevertheless, the use of this insight in defense of some punitive models of the cross generates a further problem for penal theories of the atonement. In such models God's justice and his mercy are often *pitted against one another*, with God being somehow conflicted within himself. He would love to forgive and show mercy, but his justice demands that he cannot do so and that sin must be punished. He would dearly love to simply show grace, but unfortunately he *has* to also judge. Yet one instinctively knows that this cannot be true either. God's attributes are never conflicted. Indeed, when the word "love" is applied to God, it is not used as an attribute. The phrase "God is love" describes his *being*, his ontology, and it is from this essential quality of being that all other attributes flow. So when God judges, he does so in love, and when he expresses wrath— which he undoubtedly does—it is also an expression of his essential being, which is love. Any formulations about the atonement must therefore be able to communicate God's actions within the context of his utter freedom to be himself without any internal "neediness" and his complete love that is always manifested in every action and intention.

The fourth objection to the language of satisfaction, when applied to the atonement, is its striking absence in the New Testament. The word most commonly translated as "satisfy," *chortazō*, occurs sixteen times and each occurrence refers to being "filled" in the sense of having had enough to eat. Consider, for example, Luke 6:21: "Blessed are you that hunger now, for you shall be *filled*." The word *chortazō* is *never* used in the sense of describing the satisfaction of the wrath of God or satisfying the demands of justice. If one adopts an atonement theology that insists that the wrath of God needs to be satisfied, it implies that the driving force, the engine room as it were, of the mission of Christ is the righteous anger of God. Yet the Gospel of John clearly states that this is simply not the case. It is because of the *love* of God for the world, that he sent his Son (3:16). On the cross where Jesus died, the *love* of God was satisfied, filled, and fully completed.

Finally the entire discussion about satisfaction turns around an assumed understanding of the term "sin." Once sin is defined narrowly as the breaking of a divine decree, we are immediately ushered into the law court, where legal proceedings begin. Trevor Hart suggests that when the Protestant theologians of the sixteenth and seventeenth centuries picked up the thinking of Anselm once more, there was "a tendency to conceive of the law in terms of which *iustitia* [Latin: justice] was to be defined as an abstract code akin to those of the emergent judicial administrations in Europe, and a perception of God as the absolute dispenser of such justice. Sin was chiefly a criminal offence deserving a fixed penalty, rather than the rebellious act of a prodigal provoking the burning anger of a Father's heart which is, nonetheless, never other than a form of his holy love."[3]

If too narrow a definition of the problem of humanity is used then it immediately restricts our capacity to use alternative metaphors to imagine how God interacts with the world. Yet, as we have seen, the term "sin"

3. Hart, "Redemption and Fall," 201–2.

encompasses far more than simply the breaking of a rule. Sin is a descriptive term about a state of being, rather than a set of actions or misdeeds. It includes those who have committed offenses against others, as well as those who have been offended against. It encompasses the outcasts, the excluded, the captives, the shamed. *It is a word that simply gathers up into one basket all that is out of kilter in God's created order.* It is because it is so broad in its meaning that we require a range of rich metaphors to do justice to the depth of God's reconciling work.

Shame and the Passover

Perhaps the richest metaphor, indeed the controlling metaphor, which offers a way of explaining the meaning and intention of Christ's act of self-offering on the cross, is found in the story of the Last Supper, as recounted by the Synoptic writers. Here Christ both enacts and interprets his own mission in the celebration of the Passover meal. The Passover celebration formed a vital ingredient in the perpetuation of the national memory of deliverance from Egypt and subsequent formation of "a people" who belonged to Yahweh. As the story was told and retold each year, succeeding generations were imprinted with the collective consciousness that they were indeed God's chosen people. The Passover meal was an annual, corporate re-living of an ancient story, a story so pivotal that it framed and shaped the sense of national identity. One can imagine that, in response to the question, "Who are we?" the immediate answer would have been, "We are the people whom God brought out of slavery in the land of Egypt." It was a defining narrative. Not only so, but by the time of Joshua's entry into the promised land, the remembrance of the exodus event was framed within the context of deliverance from shame. "Then the LORD said to Joshua, 'Today I have rolled away the reproach of Egypt from you.' So the place has been called Gilgal to this day" (Josh 5:9). The word that the New International Version translates here as "reproach" is *herpâ*, which means disgrace, rebuke, reproach, or shame. The experience of the Hebrews during their time of captivity in Egypt was remembered in a quite different way to the experience of captivity in Babylon many years later. In Egypt theirs was a time of reproach and disgrace, a time when they were unfairly treated as second- or even third-class citizens in a foreign land. They did not remember that period as an experience of acute guilt or disobedience to the covenant, for such a relationship was yet to be established. The miraculous deliverance by the intervention of the angel of the Lord secured their rescue, their salvation, from a profoundly shameful place.

When Jesus chose to celebrate this pivotally important meal in an upper room with his twelve apostles, he did so with the intention of reframing what it could mean. He took the simple elements of bread and wine and, instead of allowing them to refer solely back to an ancient past, declared that they now pointed to *him*. It was as if he was taking the narrative of the formation of the people of God and re-configuring it around himself. It was a bold and decisive move and one in which he was, in effect, declaring that his impending death needed to be interpreted against the backdrop of the story of deliverance from Egypt. This one metaphor, the Passover Lamb, links the story of Christ with the ancient story of Israel and was offered as the lens through which we could make sense of the events that unfolded on Calvary. During the Passover meal, as the bread and wine are shared, Jesus offers an interpretation of his actions. The bread is his broken body, the cup is his blood outpoured in a representative and sacrificial manner. It is given for others, for their benefit, on their behalf. His death would not be simply a private individual tragedy but it had sacrificial significance. Both Mark and Luke record the words of Jesus in similar fashion:

> "This is my blood of the covenant, which is poured out for many,"
> he said to them.
>
> (Mark 14:24)

> In the same way, after the supper he took the cup, saying, "This cup is the new covenant in my blood, which is poured out for you."
>
> (Luke 22:20)

Yet Matthew diverges from this formula of words when he writes,

> "This is my blood of the covenant, which is poured out for many for *the forgiveness of sins*."
>
> (Matt 26:26)

Matthew is the only evangelist who adds the phrase "for the forgiveness of sins." What did he mean by this? Was he referring to the remission of private individual guilt, the declaration that an individual may, as a result of his death, experience an inner sense of relief at having been pardoned? There may well be a sense of this individual appropriation in the words of Jesus at this point in the narrative in Matthew's Gospel, but that is probably not his primary focus. To understand Matthew's choice of phrase we must return to biblical narratives in the Old Testament in order to observe how the term "forgiveness of sins" was perceived. Many centuries after the dramatic deliverance from Egypt, Israel as a nation faced a crisis. These people—God's own people, who had been given the promised land to inhabit, who had worshipped in the holy city of Jerusalem, who had possessed the temple where God's presence was known and felt—found themselves in exile. How could this disaster be interpreted theologically, for it seemed that God's rich and abundant promises of protection and permanence had been abandoned? How could they sing the songs of Zion in a strange land—a place of shameful exile? The answer the prophets expounded was that it was because of disobedience, an abject failure to fulfill the gracious obligations of the covenant, that they found themselves away from home in a hostile land. The solution was therefore clear. As a nation they needed to experience "forgiveness of sins," for it was only via forgiveness that geographical restoration could become a reality. The "forgiveness of sins" thus became synonymous with liberation and return from exile. "Forgiveness of sins" *meant* that there was no longer a need for the nation to dwell in a place of shame. Listen to the words of Jer 33:4–11:

> For this is what the LORD, the God of Israel, says about the houses in this city and the royal palaces of Judah that have been torn down to be used against the siege ramps and the sword in the fight with the Babylonians: "They will be filled with the dead bodies of the men I will slay in my anger and wrath. I will hide my face from this city because of all its wickedness.
>
> Nevertheless, I will bring health and healing to it; I will heal my people and will let them enjoy abundant peace and security. I will bring Judah and Israel back from captivity and will rebuild them as they were before. I will cleanse them from all the sin they have committed against me *and will forgive all their sins of rebellion against me.* Then this city will bring me renown, joy, praise, and honor before all nations on earth that hear of all the good things I do for it; and they will be in awe and will tremble at the abundant prosperity and peace I provide for it."
>
> This is what the LORD says: "You say about this place, 'It is a desolate waste, without men or animals.' Yet in the towns of Judah

and the streets of Jerusalem that are deserted, inhabited by neither men nor animals, there will be heard once more the sounds of joy and gladness, the voices of bride and bridegroom, and the voices of those who bring thank-offerings to the house of the LORD, saying, 'Give thanks to the LORD Almighty, for the LORD is good; his love endures forever.' For I will restore the fortunes of the land as they were before," says the LORD.

For the Jews, "forgiveness of sins" was a phrase that evoked deep joy and hope. It could never have meant that it was simply and purely about a private individual blessing. Rather it had profound political overtones and signified the ending of the period of shameful exile. These words, spoken on the lips of Jesus at the Passover meal, heralded something momentous. In him, and through his body and blood, the forgiveness of sins would finally signify the ending of shameful exclusion and the ultimate "return from exile."[4]

This chapter began with an investigation into the meaning of the word "sacrifice," and our discussion has taken us into the medieval world of Anselm and the language of satisfaction. Let us return then to our starting point. What is the strange world of sacrifice all about? Can we confine

---

4. N. T. Wright has commented on the issue as follows:

The other great theme is, of course, forgiveness of sins. Here I want to stress a point which seems to me vital, and regularly overlooked. From the exile to Bar Kochba, and arguably beyond, exile itself was seen as the punishment for sins; so forgiveness of sins was another way of saying "end of exile." We who live in the shadow of the medieval church, of Martin Luther, of soul-searching pietism, and now of navel-gazing self-help spiritualities, have to make a huge historical effort of the imagination to get this right. Read Daniel 9, Ezekiel 34–37, Jeremiah 31, and above all Isaiah 40–55, and you will see that if exile is the result of sin, return from exile simply is the forgiveness of sins. Forgiveness, in other words, in this period isn't first and foremost a matter of private piety, of the individual wrestling with a troubled conscience. If you're in prison, being granted an amnesty doesn't mean you can feel good inside yourself. It means you are free to go home. This is all summed up in a little verse in Lamentations 4:22: "The punishment of your iniquity, O daughter Zion, is accomplished; he will keep you in exile no longer." Jesus' announcement of the kingdom, therefore, and his regular offer of forgiveness of sins, mean, in effect: this is how exile is ending! This is how God is becoming King! This is how evil is defeated! This is how Yahweh is returning to Zion! This, I submit, is thoroughly historically grounded and believable within Jesus' world. Lots of other first-century Jews thought they knew how God was becoming King, and thought they themselves would be key instruments of that kingship. Jesus belongs on that map.

http://www.ntwrightpage.com/Wright_Servant_Jesus.htm

this language to ancient primitive cultures—cultures that are interesting, no doubt, but have nothing to say to us? Anyone who is a parent automatically knows what sacrifice means. It can mean sleepless nights, loss of income, loss of leisure time, loss of identity. It means a lifetime of loving concern, often tipping over into times of great anxiety. And in moments of extremity the vast majority of parents know that they will do anything, literally anything, for the sake of their own child. This is the world of sacrifice *par excellence*, a world in which love is so deep and so passionate, that nothing other than sacrifice will be sufficient, for the sake of one's own flesh and blood. It is this image, drawn from the world of the family rather than the law court, that comes closer to the heartbeat of God's redeeming work.

Sacrifice is thus a symbolic action signifying self-donation. Taking this notion into an attempt to understand the nature of the "exchange" that took place on the cross, we witness a dual process taking place. Firstly, Christ, in his full humanity, stands before the Father as our representative. Much as an ambassador would represent an entire nation, just so Christ represents the entirety of the human race. He represents *both* the guilty—the perpetrators of violence and suffering—*and* the innocent, those who have been the victims of abuse and neglect. In his self-offering, the sacrificial offering of himself, he expresses solidarity with the tragedy of humanity, all those who have been marginalized and excluded as well as those who have been responsible for that very marginalization. In reality he takes all of us, the guilty, the shamed, the excluded, the included, the innocent, the powerless, the weak, the dominant—*all* are represented in him. His own baptism in the Jordan by John was in one sense totally unnecessary. He has no need to turn in repentance towards his Father. Yet, in another sense, it was profoundly and urgently demanded because of the pain, the tragedy, and the sheer sinfulness of humankind. His descent into those waters was his total identification, his solidarity with us.

Yet the other dimension to this self-offering was that Christ, as God, was also offering to us the very life of God. He represented the being-in-communion of the Trinity to humanity and the pouring of his blood was his life, the life of God, donated for us. It was the ultimate sign of God turning his face to us, expressing in the fullest possible way his utter commitment, his total determination to give himself in self-offering. Thus this one sacrifice was offered with a dual focus: to represent God to us and us to God. Those two offerings, given towards different objectives, meet at one point in one place on one day in the one God-man Jesus Christ. As such, it is the perfect, unique demonstration of love. Yet despite the urge to burst into a doxology of praise for this extraordinary gift, we have still not arrived at a place of resolution. We need to look at that touching point more closely, to peer into its depths, in order to discern the kind of task that Jesus Christ willingly, freely undertook.

10

Crucifixion

ALL FOUR GOSPELS TELL their stories of Jesus in such a way that the crucifixion and resurrection of Christ are the culmination of their narrative. These differing narratives weave a tale depicting the unfolding plot of the Christian faith, and it is through this story that the restoration of humankind is effected. Yet the history of Christian theology reveals a bewildering and at times highly divergent palette of interpretations as to what was actually achieved by Christ. What precisely is the nature of the disease that distorts human existence, and by what means has that disease been dealt with? Answers to these two fundamental questions often reveal theological edifices that are closely linked to particular social and cultural contexts. To point out this tendency is not necessarily to deny the validity of disparate contributions, but simply to observe that the vast range of human experience elicits a corresponding range of theological options that address differing issues. Taking the dynamic relationship between honor and shame as our starting point falls into this same pattern of searching for an appropriate point of resonance between the biblical world and our own. It is not to claim too much for the place of shame as a theological category, but merely to insist that the question of shame needs to be heard, not only because it is tragically so evident in our world today but also because it is so pervasive throughout the pages of Scripture if we but recognize it.

When approaching the question of the place of the crucifixion and resurrection in the wider narrative of the Gospels, it is my contention that there must be a "red thread" that joins the disparate stories of Jesus' encounters with the people of his day and the climactic events at the end of his life. In what way do the Gospel stories cohere together to form one narrative? The crucifixion narrative is a crucial piece of drama lying within the broader narrative of both the Incarnation of the Son and the longer story of Israel. It tells us much about the true nature of the Trinity—the Father, Son, and Spirit acting and being together—and each part of this narrative needs to be sewn together to form a coherent tapestry. The danger with much Western theology is that the crucifixion has become detached from the prior narrative of Christ—his remarkable birth, his dealings with the ordinary people of his day, his teaching, his storytelling, his interaction with his disciples and the religious and political rulers of the day. All of this must be included into the story of the crucifixion, otherwise the event of Calvary simply becomes part of a theological abstraction known as "the atonement." The question that faces us, therefore, is how to draw lines from the stories concerning the life of Jesus to the stories of his death and resurrection. In particular, we need to explore how the question of shame appears in the tales of Jesus' life and ministry and how it points to the later event of the death of Christ. If Jesus entered the place of the most profound shame on the cross, we are compelled to ask if there are any precursors of this earlier on in his ministry. Are there any clues or hints that come early in the narratives suggesting that encountering shame would be a recurrent motif leading Jesus ultimately to his own death? Could it possibly be true that the issue of honor and shame is an underlying current that ties together the loose ends and incidental occasions and makes the crucifixion take on a different hue? This is precisely what one scholar, K. C. Hanson, has claimed in his analysis of the "blessings and woes" in Matthew's Gospel.[1] He argues that in translating the original Greek word *makarios*—used repeatedly in the Beatitudes (Matt 5:3–10)—as "blessed," the primary meaning of the text is missed. Rather it should be translated as "O how honorable!" for these statements are value judgments made by the wider community upon an individual when an honorable action has been preformed. Similarly, the reproachful word *ouai*, found towards the end of Matthew's Gospel (Matt 23) and usually translated as "Woe!" is

1. Hanson, "A Cultural Analysis of Matthew."

better translated as "O how shameful!" If Hanson is right, then the way in which Matthew has chosen to present the teachings of Jesus in his Gospel is highly significant. They begin with a series of statements in chapter 5 declaring "O how honorable . . ." and conclude in chapter 23 with "O how shameful . . ." It is as if Matthew uses this rhetorical device as bookends to hold together the lengthy teaching sections in his Gospel. Honor and shame are then offered to us as the lens through which we are to read his Gospel.

Thus we need to explore whether the Gospels do in reality present us with such a portrayal of Jesus. Do his conversations with those he met on the way and his teachings reflect any emphasis on questions of honor and shame? If they do then the next question must be how such incidents inform the interpretation of his death and resurrection. The most striking thing about the earthly ministry of Jesus is that he frequently and intentionally chose to enter places of shame and associate with shamed people. He spoke to the despised Samaritan woman at the well; he spoke to and touched lepers; he had physical contact with the woman with an issue of blood; he went to the house of the despised and shamed Zacchaeus. These incidents, and many others, portray Jesus as a person who was unafraid of shame and indeed actively sought to locate himself among the shamed. It is as if Jesus did not attach significance to the shame that was generated by the culture at that time. Why was that? How was Christ able to transcend the awful power of shame and replace it with honor? To answer these questions we will take a few examples that illustrate his approach.

The Parable of the Prodigal Son

This parable appears in Luke's Gospel amidst a cluster of other parables, all of which contrive to illustrate the essence of the coming kingdom of God. The parable is thus a cameo portrait of meaning and intention of the mission of God in Christ. Are there any hints that this parable, which encapsulates the heart of the story of Jesus, contains within it telltale signs of the dynamic interplay between honor and shame? The tale opens with the outrageous demand from the younger son for his share of the inheritance that was due to him. Imagine how this would have been received by the first hearers of the story. A young man has the effrontery to demand what he could only expect to receive once his father had died. It was, in effect, a publicly expressed longing that his father should be dead. The whole village would have known about this request and immediately would have felt anger towards the young man and sympathy for the father who would have been humiliated. Yet the father astonishingly allows this request and permits the son to make a hurried sale of his estate so that he may effect a quick departure. In ceding to this request the father is, in effect, saying that he is prepared to "be dead" for the sake of his son. He is willing to endure the most painful public shaming out of love for a rebellious off-spring. In so doing he allows the son to go and leave the warm embrace of his family and his village community. The act of "letting go" is reminiscent of Paul's claim that God "gives us up" to face the consequences of our own choices (Rom 1:24). Such a giving up can only be done as an act of love, for love can never control or manipulate, but always grants freedom.

The consequences of the young man's choice are graphically detailed. After having wasted his inheritance he find himself alone and destitute, his "friends" have deserted him; he has nowhere to lay his head and is forced to find employment feeding pigs. The significance of pigs must not be lost here. Pigs were unclean animals within Jewish culture. To find oneself tending pigs is a synonym for being in the place of the most profound shame. From that point on, the son can descend no lower and even though he is desperate he hatches a plan to return to his family home to find employment as a hired hand. There is no hint yet that he returns feeling chastened and repentant. As he approaches the village, the father, who must have been watching and waiting for this day, gathers up the clothes he is wearing and runs through the village in order to embrace the son who was lost. This extraordinary action—running through the village—is not something a man over a certain age would be expected to do. But the father does not care, for his passion for the lost son is overwhelming. He is prepared to humiliate himself yet further, even though he has already been shamed by his son's departure. His unconditional embrace of the son leads to the son's recognition of his folly and his subsequent heartfelt repentance. His re-orientation back towards his father is a response to the gracious overwhelming reception that he received. It was the experience of being hugged and accepted that caused his repentance and not the other way round. Yet, even at the moment of joyous celebration, the shame of the father is not removed. The older son, whose responsibility at a public feast would have been to welcome the guests, refuses even to enter the home and prefers to wait outside. Despite the pleas of his father he will not be placated. What kind of rebelliousness is this? That even at the moment of most profound reconciliation, the older son heaps further shame on his long-suffering father? In what way does this parable throw light on the event of the cross? To the Middle Eastern listener this is a story from first to last about *shame*. The younger son shames his father by his request for money. The father allows himself to be shamed by acceding to the demand. This young man enters a place of shame when he is taken on by the pig farmer. The older son continues to shame the father even after his brother's return. This parable speaks to us about the God who suffers shame on our account. Jesus, like the father who was prepared to "be dead" for the sake of his son, was prepared to enter the place of death for us.

Jesus Anointed by a "Sinful" Woman

All four Gospels contain a story of Jesus being anointed by a woman and Matthew's account asserts that this one story will prove to be integral to any subsequent proclamation of the gospel. Matthew, Mark, and John locate the story in the home of Simon the Leper. Luke's account places the event at the home of Simon the Pharisee and it is this account that is particularly instructive for our purposes. Jesus is invited to the home of the Pharisee ostensibly as an act of generous hospitality to a respected rabbi. Yet immediately it becomes apparent that there was a hidden agenda in his invitation. Simon offers Jesus none of the expected cultural courtesies that would demonstrate respect for a guest. Jesus receives no kiss of welcome, his dusty feet are not washed, and his head is not anointed with oil. The failure to offer these symbolic gestures in front of other invited guests would have been deeply humiliating. Jesus is publicly shamed, yet chooses not to turn and leave the home but to remain in that place of shame.

Luke records that a woman who had "lived a sinful life" appears in the room. One is left to conjecture that she was a prostitute and that she had had some kind of prior experience or meeting with Jesus that had produced a remarkable transformation. She arrives at the dinner party, uninvited, yet ready with an alabaster jar of perfume. This is a planned act of lavish gratitude. Upon seeing the shaming that Jesus has endured she emerges from the shadows unable to contain herself any longer. She proceeds to anoint Jesus with her tears and her perfume, wiping his feet with her hair. To loosen her hair and then to touch a man in public with her hair was shocking. It symbolized her complete identification and commitment to the shamed person of Jesus who is here reclining at a dinner table. Jesus freely accepts that touching display from this woman and sees it as evidence that she has truly accepted the grace of God for herself. The story thus turns around the way in which Jesus enters into and remains in a place of shame. In that place he gladly accepts the touch of a shamed woman. Her act of kneeling before him in an act of gratitude demonstrated that she perceived his divine nature. His declaration that her sins were forgiven confirmed that. It is a tale that foreshadows the event of Calvary, where Jesus enters the place of the greatest shame. He willingly chose to allow himself to be taken to the most shameful place, outside the city, on a cross, in full public view, so that our shame could be absorbed in him.

The Story of Blind Bartimaeus

Exactly the same issues are addressed when Jesus encounters blind Bartimaeus (Mark 10:46–50). If an atonement theology is framed in such a way that it simply and only deals with the question of individual guilt and its aftermath, then we immediately encounter problems in interpreting the story of Bartimaeus in a coherent way. Do we simply say that he was a "sinner" included in the blanket judgment of Paul in Rom 3:23: "for all have sinned and fall short of the glory of God"? In one sense this is, of course, true, yet if we remain with the Gospel narrative as it is given to us, then that is not the primary emphasis of the story. He is described as sitting outside of the city of Jericho, stumbled upon as Jesus and his disciples were leaving. This position—outside the city gates—is significant. He remains an outsider, excluded, not welcome inside the walls of the city where there is safety, commerce, and community, but outside, compelled to feed off the scraps that society left behind or were donated to him. He sits in a place of exclusion, a place of shame. This shameful place is emphasized by the attitude of the disciples who rebuke and do not allow him a voice. Those who are shamed are not only excluded but are silenced. They have no right to speak or to be heard. His shameful status is further underlined by the name by which he is known, Bartimaeus. It is a name of Aramaic origin formed from two words, *bar*, meaning "son of" and perhaps *ṭim'ay* meaning "foul" or "unclean." His name, "son of filth,"[2] was a taunt used by locals to further heap disgrace upon him. So the pausing of Jesus to pay attention to this poor beggar was a revolutionary pause. In that one gesture he signals that this outsider is noticed, his voice has been heard, his request taken seriously. Jesus refuses to be constrained or influenced by the cultural expectations of his day; he rejects the commonly accepted definitions of who is an insider and who is not. Bartimaeus is not at this moment defined in terms of his guilt, but rather by his shameful exclusion. Jesus effectively looks at the shame of this man and counts it as nothing. He scorns it (Heb 12:2) and in so doing prefigures all that he will ultimately accomplish on the cross. His action was both intensely personal—in that poor Bartimaeus received his sight—and simultaneously profoundly political. If this man, this blind beggar, this complete nobody, is to be included now into the very fabric of normal society, then this demands a complete overhaul of the way in which society is structured.

The Woman Caught in Adultery

We witness this again in the story where Jesus is presented with the woman caught in the act of adultery in John 8.

> The teachers of the law and the Pharisees brought in a woman caught in adultery. They made her stand before the group and said to Jesus, "Teacher, this woman was caught in the act of adultery. In the Law Moses commanded us to stone such women. Now what do you say?" They were using this question as a trap, in order to have a basis for accusing him.
>
> But Jesus bent down and started to write on the ground with his finger. When they kept on questioning him, he straightened up and said to them, "If any one of you is without sin, let him be the first to throw a stone at her." Again he stooped down and wrote on the ground.
>
> At this, those who heard began to go away one at a time, the older ones first, until only Jesus was left, with the woman still standing there. Jesus straightened up and asked her, "Woman, where are they? Has no one condemned you?"
>
> "No one, sir," she said.

2. Strong's Concordance, Entry 924; Bailey, *Jesus through Middle Eastern Eyes*, 173.

"Then neither do I condemn you," Jesus declared. "Go now and leave your life of sin"

(John 8:3–11)

It is an intriguing account. The woman has been found out, she is clearly guilty for she has been caught in the act, and she is now brought before Jesus as a kind of legal test case. Would Jesus uphold the Torah and have her stoned to death or not? If he did not keep the letter of the law the Pharisees would know that he was an impostor, a trickster and rabble-rouser posing as a rabbi. If he did insist upon her execution then his revolutionary message of the arrival of the kingdom, his entire mission in effect, would be placed in jeopardy, as he would appear to be no different from the Pharisees themselves. Either way Jesus would come out the loser—or so they assumed. The astonishing feature of this account is not so much the words of Jesus, although they are indeed searching and exposing, but rather his actions. The woman is brought before him and is placed in the center of a circle, standing. One can easily imagine the threatening and humiliating position she is placed in. Jesus then bends down to write on the ground. In so doing he makes himself lower than her. She is compelled to look down to where Jesus is squatting as he writes with his finger in the sand. All of the actions of Jesus were intentional and all of them, together with his teaching, conspire to illustrate something new about the nature of the kingdom that he came to announce. So his bending down in front of her is a prophetic action with revolutionary intent. Here is a clear case of adultery and the woman is paraded in public, thereby exposing her to shame, yet Jesus bends down before her, making himself lower than her, thus immediately shifting the focus of attention from her shame to his chosen position beneath her. It is an action that speaks about his desire to remove the shame from such people, while at the same time taking her guilt and that of those who accused her seriously.

The Sermon on the Mount

Not only are the personal encounters and parables of Jesus either directly or implicitly dealing with shamed people, but much of his ethical teaching carries the same motif. Although Matthew does not use the words "shame" or "honor" in the Sermon on the Mount (Matt 5–7), an appreciation of the cultural context within which he was living reveals that shame and honor are the hidden forces that constrain or motivate behavior. We will look in some detail at Matt 5:38–42 to demonstrate this.

> You have heard that it was said, "Eye for eye, and tooth for tooth." But I tell you, Do not resist an evil person. If someone strikes you on the right cheek, turn to him the other also. And if someone wants to sue you and take your tunic, let him have your cloak as well. If someone forces you to go one mile, go with him two miles. Give to the one who asks you, and do not turn away from the one who wants to borrow from you.

Jesus here addresses the question of how to respond to the presence of oppressive, humiliating practices, a subject close to the heart of the poor of his day who were all too used to the actions of the occupying power from Rome. In doing so he deploys three examples: being struck on the face, the demand for a tunic in a legal case, and the Roman practice of pressing peasants into service in carrying heavy loads. All three scenarios were familiar, everyday occurrences and the source of much anguish and frustration. What does Jesus offer such people as an example to those who wish to know what it means to live within the kingdom of God that Jesus claimed he came to bring? Let us take each scenario in turn.

In Middle Eastern culture striking someone on the face was not only an aggressive act, but also one designed in shame. In order for someone to strike an opponent on the right cheek, it would have been necessary to use the back of the right hand to do so. The left hand was only used for sanitary purposes and a backhanded slap was not capable of caus-ing serious injury. It was merely intended to humiliate, as it indicated, symbolically, an unequal relationship. The aggressor giving the slap with the back of the hand demonstrated by his action that he considered his victim to be of a lower social status. How does Jesus advise such a person to react? He simply says turn the other cheek—namely the left cheek. Now the aggressor is faced with a dilemma. How can he strike the person on the left cheek? He can no longer do so with the back of his hand, yet if he uses his fist, he tacitly concedes that his victim is his equal. Surely he does not want to do that? Turning the left cheek thus communicates in a non-verbal way that the victim refuses to be shamed by the initial slap. He simply will not accept the designation of one who is humiliated but instead turns the tables on the aggressor who now has to choose whether to accept the dignity that his "victim" is displaying. It is a non-violent way of diffusing a potentially inflammatory situation and its potency turns around the question of shame and honor.

The second illustration including the poor person and the tunic involves the same dynamic. Indebtedness in first-century Palestine was endemic. A highly stratified society with a tiny minority of wealthy land-lords and a vast majority of peasants living in penury produced deep resentments and the feeling of utter powerlessness. If the rains failed or if there was a sudden hailstorm or a plague of blight appeared, then a whole year's harvest could be wiped out and the poor tenant farmer left with no income and a demanding landlord breathing down his neck. It is hardly surprising that many of Jesus' parables tell of people who have fallen into debts that they find impossible to repay. Into this context Jesus speaks. If someone sues you for the non-payment of a debt and insists on taking your tunic as surety, what response is possible? According to the Torah there were strict rules about the taking of a tunic. "If you take your neighbor's cloak as a pledge, return it to him by sunset, because his cloak is the only covering he has for his body. What else will he sleep in? When he cries out to me, I will hear, for I am compassionate" (Exod 22:26–27). Only the very poor would have nothing to offer a creditor but their outer garment, but the law said that if this is demanded it must be returned by nightfall. Jesus takes this precedent and builds upon it. One is left to imag-ine the demeaning action of a ruthless landlord who comes and demands the poor peasant's cloak. There is a deep shame incurred in such an act. Why then does Jesus counsel his hearers to offer their cloak as well? Hear how Walter Wink answers this question.

> This would mean stripping off all their clothing and marching out of court stark naked! Imagine the guffaws this saying must have evoked! There stands the creditor, covered in shame, the poor debtor's outer garment in one hand, his undergarment in the other. The tables have been turned on the creditor. The debtor had no hope of winning the case; the law was entirely in the creditor's favor. But the poor man has transcended this attempt to humiliate him. He has risen above the shame. At the same time he has regis-tered a stunning protest against the system that created his debt.[3]

The third illustration is taken from the Roman practice of *anagareia*, or impressed labor. According to Roman law, when a Roman battalion

3. Wink, *Engaging the Powers*, 179.

was on the move, they were permitted to compel local peasants to carry their loads up to, but no further than, one mile. If a Roman soldier were to abuse this limitation and take advantage of defenseless citizens, severe sanctions could be imposed upon him. Jesus speaks to his hearers about this hated practice. What should they do when they are humiliated by this demand? The answer of Jesus is typically surprising: offer to carry the soldiers pack an extra mile, voluntarily. Why is this a solution? In doing so the poor peasant is again refusing to accept the shame that has just been loaded onto his shoulders. Instead he offers with dignity to go beyond the distance that was permitted under the *anagareia* regulations. If the soldier accepted this offer, he knew he would be in breach of his commanding officer's rules and he dare not risk incurring a penalty. If, on the other hand, he refused to accept the offer of an additional mile, he would immediately have restored the poor peasant's honor. Again it is a brilliant piece of non-violent resistance in which the threat of being shamed is turned around against the aggressor and the oppressive environment simply evaporates. These examples conspire to push our investigation further towards the climax of the story of Jesus. In each Gospel narrative we have witnessed the question of shame emerging time and again. It demands to be noticed and taken seriously as a persistent and perennial "disease" affecting both individuals and society alike. We have seen how it distorts human relationships, divides communities, and contributes to the rupture of the relationship between humankind and God. The entire ministry of Jesus has pointed towards a final showdown with shame and the events surrounding the crucifixion are simply the continuation of this recurring theme.

The Garden of Gethsemane

As Jesus approached the moment of crucifixion, we read the moving story of his time of agonized prayer in the garden of Gethsemane. It is a vital story that we must include in our collection of tales that together tell of the way in which God seeks to bring about reconciliation. The details of the time in this garden are well rehearsed. He takes some trusted disciples with him to be a source of strength and encouragement, while he wrestles in prayer before the day of dread that awaits him. As Christ enters more deeply into prayer he falls to his knees and cries out "may this cup be taken from me." His forthcoming ordeal, about which he has talked with his disciples and forewarned them, is about to reach its denouement. He will be subjected to an unjust trial and scourged and then taken to the place of greatest shame. This experience is described by Jesus as "a cup that he has to drink." What, however, was the content of this cup that was so horrific that even Christ, the beloved Son of the Father, recoiled from?

The symbolism of "the cup" is multifaceted. Sometimes the metaphor of "cup" denotes overflowing joy, as the Psalmist exclaims in Ps 23—"my cup overflows." At other times the meaning of the metaphor of "cup" is entirely different. We see this, for example, in the apocalyptic book of Revelation—written in "code" to encourage a persecuted and oppressed Christian church, traumatized by the might of the Roman Empire—where the writer states, "God remembered Babylon the Great and gave her the cup filled with the wine of the fury of his wrath." It was a statement asserting that God's righteous judgment would fall on a cruel and repressive regime, one which repeatedly failed to recognize the dignity and worth of its own citizens. On the occasion of the Last Supper Jesus lifts the cup and declares to his disciples that this represented the new covenant in his own blood. It is a cup from which they, the disciples, are invited to drink in order to symbolically declare their willingness to share in a similar fate to his. It is likely that as he spoke those words, Christ was drawing on the prophetic tradition of Zechariah.

> Rejoice greatly, O Daughter of Zion! Shout, Daughter of Jerusalem! See, your king comes to you, righteous and having salvation, gentle and riding on a donkey, on a colt, the foal of a donkey. I will take away the chariots from Ephraim and the warhorses from Jerusalem, and the battlebow will be broken. He will proclaim peace to the nations. His rule will extend from sea to sea and from the River to the ends of the earth. As for you, because of the blood of my covenant with you, I will free your prisoners from the waterless pit. Return to your fortress, O prisoners of hope; even now I announce that I will restore twice as much to you.

(Zech 9:9–12)

This passage, with the evocative image of a king entering Jerusalem on a donkey, had only just been prophetically enacted by Jesus during his entry into Jerusalem. It is a text that speaks of the liberation of prisoners from wastelands, the arrival of hope, and the proclamation of peace to the nations. All of this is to be brought into effect through the blood of the covenant, a theme that resonates with the original deliverance from Egypt. The gift of Jesus' own lifeblood would now achieve the same purpose and those who are imprisoned, captive, oppressed, and shamed would be offered liberty through the giving over of his own life.

The "cup" that Christ recoiled from in Gethsemane was offered to a different recipient. The story does not suggest that this cup contained his own blood, which would turn the whole crucifixion into a kind of bizarre ritual in which the victim sheds his own blood in fatal sacrifice and then, just prior to death, is obliged to drink it. Rather, the contents of Christ's "cup" must have been metaphorical in nature. To guide our reflections we can draw on two earlier stories that depict the purpose and scope of Christ's mission. The first is the story of Jesus visiting the home of Zacchaeus in Luke 19: Zacchaeus was a well-known, unscrupulous tax collector. His practice of extortion had earned him no friends and he lived a solitary, excluded life on the margins of society. He was one of those people who were lumped together by the Pharisees as bearing the label "tax collectors and sinners." As such, he was without doubt one who dwelt in the place of shame. It is specifically to his home, however, that Jesus chooses to go and spend time. At the conclusion of their conversation Zacchaeus experiences a complete reversal of orientation and in exuberant response throws open his hitherto closed home and offers restitution to those whom he has cheated. On witnessing this, Jesus explains that it is precisely to such people as Zacchaeus that he came into this world. He came to seek and to save the lost and this despised tax collector was a member of that group of lost souls. He has now tasted the elixir of salvation. This was always the purpose of Jesus' mission—to find those who are experiencing "lostness" and to liberate them from that place of captivity.

That this is so is evident when we recall the story of Jesus' first day of public ministry as recorded in Luke chapter 4. He returns to his hometown of Nazareth, enters the synagogue on the Sabbath, and in the midst of the service goes to the front to read from the prophet Isaiah. "The Spirit of the Lord is on me, because he has anointed me to preach good news to the poor. He has sent me to proclaim freedom for the prisoners and recovery of sight for the blind, to release the oppressed, to proclaim the year of the Lord's favor." The sermon that followed this reading is remarkable in its brevity. He simply says: "Today this scripture is fulfilled in your hearing." This deliberate action was chosen by Jesus to be his moment of disclosure. Here was his opportunity to present the entire manifesto of his mission, couched in terms of offering healing and liberation to those who are poor or captive or oppressed. It is in essence no different from what he says succinctly after his encounter with Zacchaeus, that his entire purpose can be summed by saying that he came to liberate lost people. And that lostness could be manifested in a huge variety of ways: those who are guilty of extortion, those who are poor, those who experience oppression or abuse. These two stories taken together enable us to imagine what is the content of that cup from which Christ shrank away. The cup is filled with our lostness. It is full of the sin, the shame, the violence, the guilt, and the neglect that so distorts and pollutes our world. This is the cup that contains the sum total of human misery and rebelliousness. This is the cup that Christ in that garden was faced with. The apostle Paul articulates no less in his Second Letter to the Corinthians.

> Therefore, if anyone is in Christ, he is a new creation; the old has gone, the new has come! All this is from God, who reconciled us to himself through Christ and gave us the ministry of reconciliation, that God was reconciling the world to himself in Christ, not counting men's sins against them. And he has committed to us the message of reconciliation . . . Be reconciled to God. God made him who had no sin to be sin for us, so that in him we might become the righteousness of God.

(2 Cor 5:17–21)

When Christ drank that cup he "became sin for us." He absorbed it, soaked it up, digested it. It was through his physical body that he accomplished this and not in some higher spiritual realm. One small detail contained in the Gospel accounts of the crucifixion is highly pertinent to this exploration. Towards the final moments of his crucifixion Christ experiences thirst. He cries out for his thirst to be relieved, but instead of being offered refreshing water he receives only vinegar. But how could it have been other? His task on that cross was to drink, out of sheer love, that cup of lostness, and so the vinegar that he was offered merely served to symbolize precisely what he was accomplishing at that moment. That drink did nothing to soothe the agony, but only served to symbolize the extent of it. As Christ drinks the cup to its dregs he becomes so polluted by it that it takes him down into death itself. There, on Holy Saturday, he awaits the powerful, resurrecting work of the Holy Spirit.

After the contemplation of the cup that he was about to drink, we read that an armed group who had been searching for him among the olive groves approaches Jesus. They approach him full of authority and bravado, knowing that they had the power to do what they wished with him. Jesus seizes the initiative when the guards approach. Yet, when questioned about his identity Jesus utters the simple remark, "I am he" (John 18:5), and his captors find that their supposed superiority immediately melts away for they draw back and fall to the ground. For Jesus to use such a theologically loaded phrase, "I am," was a calm declaration of the honor that was inherently his. The bodily response of his aggressors in falling to the ground reverses the expected positions of honor and shame. It is an ironic incident in which the anticipated exchange of honor and shame is suddenly reversed. The early first-century reader of this story would have been astonished. After his capture in the garden, the guards continue the process. "Prophesy! Who hit you?" they cry to the blindfolded Jesus (Luke 22:64). The humiliation intensifies with the scourging and beating and culminates in the mocking ceremony of a regal crown and stately purple robe being presented to him. These tragic, searingly painful, ironic symbols of majesty pour scorn on the claim of Christ to be a king of the Jews. His shameful treatment can lead in only one direction, towards the place of ultimate shame, death by crucifixion on a hill outside of the city.

Shame and the Crucifixion in the Writings of Paul

If triumph over shame is, as we have observed, a recurring theme in the Gospels, then we ought to expect the same theme to surface in the writings of the apostle Paul. In his First Letter to the Corinthian church he writes to a divided church. Gentile Greek-speaking Christians, steeped in the tradition of Greek philosophy, rhetoric, and oratory, mingled with Jewish Christians who were formed and shaped through Hebrew cultural practices and theology. Both groups needed to grapple with the significance of a Christ figure that had been arrested and crucified like so many thousands of other subversives in the era of Roman domination. So how was this one crucifixion different from all others? Why attach any lasting significance to *this* death? How does this obscure execution address questions that the Greek-speaking world posed, questions concerning the acquisition of honor through displays of eloquent oratory in public forums in which the benefits of *sophia* (wisdom) could be presented? Furthermore, how did it also address the concerns of those with a Jewish heritage who longed to see the evident reality of the power of God on earth? They longed to know that they would not be put to shame, yet their search took them in a very different direction. For them to know that God was present, in power, in their midst, with his face turned towards them, was sufficient for them to conclude that they belonged to the covenant of God's grace and thus were held in the place of honor. Both groups desired the same outcome, but each with vastly differing expectations of how that outcome could be realized. To these utterly different groups Paul writes: "Jews demand miraculous signs and Greeks look for wisdom, but we preach Christ crucified: a stumbling-block to Jews and foolishness to Gentiles, but to those whom God has called, both Jews and Greeks, Christ the power of God and the wisdom of God" (1 Cor 1:22–24).

In what way, however, could this crucified Christ, this stumbling block, address the vital concerns of each group? Paul resorts to the language of the Passover lamb to make his point. He writes to the divided, tetchy, Corinthian church, "Get rid of the old yeast that you may be a new batch without yeast—as you really are. For Christ, our Passover lamb, has been sacrificed" (1 Cor 5:7). Here Paul too is constructing a bridge between Christ's sacrifice on the cross and the event of the deliverance from Egypt as told in the book of Exodus. The early story must be used in an illustrative way to enable us, the readers of Paul's letters, to make sense of the cross. What then was the story of the Passover about? There we read of the oppressed Hebrews compelled to work as slaves for the might of the Egyptian empire. Their dramatic rescue through the courageous intervention of Moses is effected ultimately through the sacrificial lambs whose blood is sprinkled on the doorposts of their homes. It is because of this blood sacrifice that the angel of the Lord passes over the Hebrew homes and initiates their deliverance. This event in Jewish history is used as a paradigm through which we are invited to view the sacrifice of Christ on the cross. Christ is presented as our pascal lamb that effects our deliverance today. In order to understand this metaphor we need to apprehend correctly the meaning of that first deliverance from Egypt. The sacrificial lambs were needed to symbolize those who belonged to the people of

Yahweh. These people were oppressed, enslaved, exiled in a foreign land, under a cruel monarchy. They were, in effect, in a place of great shame. The extraordinary miracle of deliverance addressed this primary crisis. That first Passover lamb was not presented as a guilt offering made so that the Hebrews could experience forgiveness. It was *not*, initially at least, the means by which God effects the removal of guilt. Rather, it was a sacrifice offered to bring about a rescue from the place of shame, for a people who had endured much suffering. The Passover lamb thus became symbolic, in Jewish tradition, of liberation from oppression. This motif of liberty was crucial to the meaning of metaphor for that divided Corinthian church. "Do you not realize," writes Paul in effect, "that you are now to live in the place of liberty rather than in the place of shameful captivity? Think of the way in which that first Passover lamb was the ignition for the journey out of Egypt. Let that metaphor ignite your Christian lives today."

Exactly the same issue of overcoming shame is addressed by Paul in his Letter to the Romans. Many commentators regard Paul's Letter to the Romans as the fruit of many years of reflection on the nature and extent of the gospel. It was probably written in Corinth during a time of relative peace in the midst of an arduous schedule of traveling around the Mediterranean churches. It is therefore considered to be his summary of the whole gospel, covering as it does the issue of both the continuity with Jewish messianic expectations and simultaneously the radical discontinuity with much of the Jewish tradition. One might expect, therefore, that the paradigm of "guilt and forgiveness," which has so dominated theological thinking for centuries, particularly in the West, would be clearly laid out for all to see. It is surprising, to say the least, that such language is almost completely absent from the letter. At no point does Paul speak in terms of forgiveness and in only one sentence is there any reference to guilt.[4] In the light of this evidence one is compelled to come to the conclusion that Paul was operating under a different paradigm altogether.

A clue to this alternative paradigm is offered in the opening few sentences of his letter, although it is easy for us, living as we do at such a distance from the original circumstances of the letter, to miss the impact of Paul's shocking use of the Greek language. Paul begins his letter by ex-

---

4. "Now we know that whatever the law says, it says to those who are under the law, so that every mouth may be silenced and the whole world held accountable [*hupodikos*] to God" (Rom 3:19).

plaining that his vocation is to bring the liberating message of the gospel of Jesus Christ to everyone, whatever his or her ethnic background. He writes to the fledgling church in Rome, a collection of Christian communities scattered throughout the city and composed of Jewish converts, slaves, Gentiles, and the sophisticated elite of Roman society. Within Greco-Roman culture clear boundary lines were drawn between those who were honored and those who did not or could not receive honor. This relatively newly founded Christian community in Rome was steeped in this surrounding culture, a culture characterized by a fierce competitiveness, stemming from a fear of being found to be without honor. The only way to ensure that one's honor was maintained and protected was to boast of one's achievements, and to put others down who might threaten one's status. It was a brutal world, where only those with the right connections, the right education, and sufficient financial means could survive.

Scholars have shown that the entire machinery of the Roman Empire—founded upon the complex interplay of sheer force, patronage, and propaganda—was held together by an underlying dynamic of honor and shame.[5] There was an expectation that honor should be given to those who positioned themselves higher up the social pyramid. In fact, the "duty of honor" was more important than the "duty of obedience."[6] Into this world the gospel was introduced and it immediately began to subvert the foundations upon which society was built. One of the groups that belonged to the category of "the shamed" was the "barbarians." It was a term applied pejoratively to the non-Greek speaking (and, by implication, uncivilized) peoples. The New International Version has sanitized its translation of Rom 1:14 when it renders the verse, "I am bound both to Greeks and *non-Greeks*, both to the wise and the foolish." Yet the Greek word that Paul uses for "non-Greeks" is the word *barbaros*, an abusive term comparable in our day to the term "nigger." It was a term coined to describe those unruly tribes not yet under the orbit of Roman rule. Their language sounded foreign and obscure to the sophisticated Romans—a mere babbling of infantile sounds ("babbababba")—hence the pejorative "barbarians." If the verse was translated more colloquially as "I am bound both to the sophisticated and the niggers, the educated and the stupid," then we would catch something of the flavor of Paul's language. As Jewett

5. Lendon, *Empire of Honour*, 13.
6. Jewett, *Romans*, 49.

has stated, "Barbarians were considered sub-human and incapable of being civilized."[7] One of the lands that was considered to be the home of the most barbaric of peoples was Spain, yet it is to this very region that Paul wished to travel in order to take the liberating gospel (Rom 15:24). Would the church in Rome be willing to support him in this venture? That is the key question that unlocks the purpose behind this most theological of Paul's letters. If the Roman church were to be able to unequivocally join him in this missionary venture then they would need to be deeply and profoundly conscious of the way in which the gospel of Jesus Christ both subverts and inverts the prevailing culture of honor and shame. Paul goes on to describe the priorities of his mission, "first for the Jew, then for the Gentile." In so doing he cuts across the prejudices of the educated elite of Roman society who considered themselves vastly superior to the Jewish race. This good news will go to the Jews *first* and only afterwards to the other nations! We are forced then by the sheer brutal power of Paul's rhetoric to ask why he opens his letter in this way. Why does he set out to antagonize and provoke by deploying offensive language?

The answer may lie towards the end of his letter to the Romans. He explains in chapter 15 that the gospel is good news for everyone—even those outside of the Jewish faith. This notion is not in reality a new idea, for he is able to cite both the Psalms and Isaiah showing that the "nations," or the Gentiles, will one day sing the praises of Yahweh. To this end Paul feels the overwhelming vocation to take this good news to the Gentiles and writes that he wishes to travel to Spain to achieve his goal. "I plan to do so when I go to Spain. I hope to visit you while passing through and to have you assist me on my journey there, after I have enjoyed your company for a while" (Rom 15:24). He has made his plans for this journey, yet wishes to include the church in Rome in this missionary venture. How could he summon their support if it meant giving away the grace of God to those who were considered to be heathens, barbarians, Gentiles? He begins his letter by declaring that those who have received grace are now called to pass it on to those outside the Jewish faith (Rom 1:5). Paul was acutely aware of the divisive nature of Roman society and yet he boldly strides across these accepted boundary lines, claiming that the gospel of Jesus Christ subverts the entire social system. This inclusive gospel is, however, for Paul, not a source of shame as he so confidently asserts, "I

7. Ibid., 53.

am not ashamed of the gospel, because it is the power of God that brings salvation to everyone who believes" (Rom 1:16). The Greek word that he uses here for ashamed is *epaischunomai* and it is a compound word meaning, "to place a sense of disfigurement or disgrace upon someone." It is to load someone with a burden of disrepute and revulsion. Paul says that when he associates himself with the gospel of Jesus Christ, which to some is nonsense and to others is abhorrent, he feels absolutely no disfigurement at all. Robert Jewett in his commentary on the book of Romans states that this declaration "sets the tone for the entire letter"[8] and is the key text which unlocks the setting in which the letter was composed. By making this declaration Paul invites his readers in the church in Rome to view both themselves and the gospel in the same light. Paradoxically, true honor and the removal of shame are found in the life, death, and resurrection of one man who had died an ignominious death in a small province of the Roman Empire. To quote Jewett again, "There were deeply engrained social reasons why Paul should have been ashamed to proclaim such a gospel; his claim not to be ashamed signals that a social and ideological revolution has been inaugurated by the gospel."[9]

After these opening explosive verses, Paul continues in his letter to articulate the radical implications of the coming of Christ into the world. In chapter 12 he writes that the community is to take the lead in honoring one another in brotherly love (Rom 12:10) as a key distinctive and defining mark of their Christian discipleship. Again, it is hard for us to appreciate the force of his words. The Greek word that he uses here— *proēgeomai*—carries the sense that each person is to compete not in putting others down but rather in showing honor to others. And to whom is this honor to be shown? He tells us in verse 16: "not setting your minds on exalted things but being drawn towards *lowly people.*" For Paul, the meaning of the gospel was not to be understood primarily as a private, individual, and inner experience of the grace of God in Christ. This is how the gospel has been interpreted for centuries in the Western world. Instead, the gospel was to have a far more subversive impact. The entire way in which Roman culture was organized and managed was now under threat from this tiny, irrelevant, Christian community that based its hope on the death and resurrection of an unknown peasant from Israel. Instead

8. Ibid., 136.
9. Ibid., 137.

of competing against one another for honor, the Christian community was to practice the exact opposite. They were to compete in giving honor to the lowest within society, to search for those who had been shamed, ignored, bypassed, and forgotten. It is those people that the church had to seek out and in so doing invert their hopeless world, showering them with the grace that provides honor without charge. For the apostle Paul, Christ's mission was profoundly pertinent in addressing a brutal society that felt no qualms in leaving the shamed to suffer on their own. The gospel was such good news because these lost people could be found, healed, and restored and their honor was derived not from anything that they possessed or achieved but simply and only because they could stand before the face of Jesus Christ with their heads held high. In the light of all this, the question is then posed to the Roman community—"I am going to take the gospel to Spain; will you support me in this?" Their answer to this one key question would reveal much about the extent of their understanding of the revolutionary way in which the story of Jesus addresses the question of shame and honor.

Shame and the Crucifixion in 1 Peter

Paul is not alone amongst the biblical writers to take up the theme of the inversion of the shame and honor system through the power of the cross. The Apostle Peter in his First Letter addresses the scattered congregations of northern Asia Minor, attempting to encourage them to become a community of grace that expressed a true belonging to one another. His letter contains within it clues that suggest that these early Christian communities were suffering deep humiliation for their faith. In the culture of that period there was a complex interweaving of social, political, and religious practices. It was expected that honorable, pious people would pay their respects to the local deities whenever that was demanded of them. The members of the Christian communities refused to participate in such practices and when questioned about this unusual behavior might well have declared that such deities were, in fact, not deities at all but merely man-made idols. One can only imagine the hostile reaction from their neighbors that this would have elicited. How does the apostle Peter write a pastoral letter to such vulnerable Christian communities to encourage them to hold on to their newfound faith in the face of hostility and public humiliation? He opens his letter with the intriguing phrase "God's elect, strangers in the world" (1 Pet 1:1). In doing so he acknowledges, right at the outset, that these Christian brothers and sisters no longer feel that they "belong" to the communities in which they live. Although they are ethnically and linguistically no different from their neighbors they have begun to experience the reproaches of those outside of the Christian community such that they now feel themselves to be "aliens" in their own villages and towns. The excluding effects of being shamed are once again manifested. Over time the growing Christian churches had become the objects of scorn and ridicule, which is why Peter found it necessary to write in his letter, "Live such good lives among the pagans that, though they accuse you of doing wrong, they may see your good deeds and glorify God on the day he visits us" (1 Pet 2:12). The word translated here as "accuse" is *katalaleo*, which means, "to slander." When these early Christians chose to abstain from some of the normal expected cultural conventions, their bewildered neighbors resorted to various forms of verbal abuse, thereby destroying their social standing within the community. The temptation for those who were suffering in this way was to interpret their trials as "strange" or "abnormal," as if God had somehow abandoned them to their fate. Peter attempts to re-define "strangeness" and asserts that the previous set of values by which they had lived was, in God's sight, "strange" and that now their sufferings were nothing to be ashamed about (1 Pet 4:16). DeSilva articulates Peter's thinking in this way.

> The author is trying to tell people who might all too easily interpret the experience of loss, pain, and suffering as a sign of divine displeasure that God is not in the reproaches and abuse of the unbelievers punishing the sufferers, but *with* the believers in the midst of their experiences of hostility and resistance. It was God who provided for their redemption from a futile way of life, dissociation from which is the cause of their present suffering (1:19). Their suffering "in accordance with God's will" means they are moving in the direction that God wants for them, even though their neighbors are responding with hostility.[10]

How then could these disparate, suffering, and disgraced groups become a true Christian community? Only by being built upon the same foundation stone. Peter writes: "For in Scripture it says: 'See, I lay a stone

---

10. deSilva, *Turning Shame into Honor*, 173–74.

in Zion, a chosen and precious cornerstone, and the one who trusts in him will never be put to shame'" (1 Pet 2:6), which is a quotation from Isa 28:16 which states, "So this is what the Sovereign LORD says: 'See, I lay a stone in Zion, a tested stone, a precious cornerstone for a sure foundation; the one who trusts will never be dismayed.'" Peter declares that Christ had endured the ignominy of public execution yet had reversed its effects. The cross has become a source of true honor in the sight of God, and so for all those who place their trust in this cornerstone, shame is removed.

Shame and the Crucifixion in Hebrews

The writer of the book of Hebrews likewise deals with the issue of how the crucifixion of Christ addresses the question of removing the burden of shame from despised people and replacing it with honor. The letter begins with a depiction of the glory that inherently belongs to the Son of God. The term "glory" (*doxa*) is often paired with "honor" (*timē*) in the New Testament. They appear together as bedfellows and as the exact antithesis of shame. The apostle Paul uses this rhetorical technique repeatedly in his Letter to the Romans, where he insists that the result of being found "in Christ" is that "glory, honor, and peace" are conferred (Rom 2:7, 10). When the writer uses such terms in his letter, we need to be alert to the particular sensitivity of such phrases. In a culture that was as highly stratified and competitive as the Mediterranean culture of the first century, any references to honor and glory would immediately provoke interest. So the letter does not hesitate in insisting at the very outset that the Son is the radiance of God's glory and that he now sits at the right hand of the majesty in heaven (1:3). The usage of the term "the right hand" is deliberate. The right hand was the honored hand in comparison to the left hand, and those who attended feasts and sat at the right hand of the host occupied the most honored position.[11] Having outlined to his readers the honored and glorious place that the crucified and shamed Christ now occupies, the writer goes on to state that it is the intention of the Father to bring many into this place of glory too (Heb 2:10). Although we are merely eavesdropping on a distant conversation and can only fully hear one voice in that conversation, it is clear that questions of honor and shame are very live

---

11. E.g., "Exalted to the right hand of God, he has received from the Father the promised Holy Spirit and has poured out what you now see and hear" (Acts 2:33).

topics in the Christian community to which the letter was written. It is as if the pressing issue being addressed concerns how one can hold one's head up high with dignity as a follower of Christ in a society that militated against every value that Jesus Christ espoused.

One of the ways in which this beleaguered Christian community could maintain a sense of honor was through an appeal to an alternative set of values. These values, embodied in the church community, could sustain its members and it was because of this key support mechanism that the writer urges his readers not to give up meeting together (Heb 10:25). Through this avenue of mutual support their sense of honor could be maintained in the midst of a hostile society. Yet the writer knows that this human support alone is not sufficient and he needs therefore to point to the way in which the awful question of shame was dealt a final blow in the crucifixion of Christ. The key phrase in the whole argument is found in 12:2 where we read, "Let us fix our eyes on Jesus, the author and perfecter of our faith, who for the joy set before him endured the cross, scorning its shame, and sat down at the right hand of the throne of God." This sentence comes at the conclusion of a lengthy passage in the letter in which the writer has shown himself acutely aware of the way in which this Christian community had suffered at the hands of the surrounding, dominant culture. He enumerates the way in which this has happened in 10:32–34: "Remember those earlier days after you had received the light, when you endured in a great conflict full of suffering. Sometimes you were publicly exposed to insult and persecution; at other times you stood side by side with those who were so treated. You suffered along with those in prison and joyfully accepted the confiscation of your property, because you knew that you yourselves had better and lasting possessions."

What the writer highlights here is the way in which Christians had been made into a public spectacle (*theatrizō*). They had been paraded in full view of the local community, laughed at, scorned, ridiculed, exposed to insult, and publicly shamed. This is what happens in any society where there is a competitive hierarchy of honor and shame. There have to be winners and losers and this must be demonstrated in the public arena. These poor early Christians had suffered in this shameful way and their plight is taken up by the writer of this letter. His response is to list all those heroes of the faith (chapter 11) who had also suffered such public persecution and shaming. At the end of the list the writer explains how all of them had been hated and excluded by society for their faith; they were "destitute, persecuted, and mistreated—the world was not worthy of them. They wandered the deserts and mountains, and in caves and holes in the ground" (Heb 11:37–38). Here is a depiction of the most profound forms of shaming, for these heroes no longer had homes to dwell in, no place to call their own, no recognition of their full humanity. They had been stripped of anything that gave them dignity and honor, yet their faith had enabled them to persevere.

The argument of the writer then moves on to the case of Jesus himself. Jesus belongs to this line of shamed "heroes." He too was excluded, mocked, and ridiculed; he too had no place to lay his head at night; he too was finally stripped of any semblance of dignity and raised up on a cross outside the city walls. And there, precisely at that place of ultimate shaming, Christ looks upon the shame that he is enduring. The writer uses a word which is usually translated as "scorn" (*kataphroneō*) and which literally means "to think against," or "to despise," to consider as nothing at all. It is a powerful rhetorical device to assert that Christ on the cross was, in effect, *shaming shame*. The moment of crucifixion is thus depicted as the entering into the place of shame in order to rob shame of its power to humiliate. This entrance is more than simply exemplary. It is done "*for us*" and "*with us*." This is the force of the argument on Heb 2:10 where the writer speaks about the way in which Christ would taste death for everyone, for "in bringing many sons and daughters to glory, it was fitting that God, for whom and through whom everything exists, should make the pioneer of their salvation perfect through what he suffered." The acuteness of the suffering of Christ was, in human terms, the endurance of the most intense shaming. Yet this shaming has now been rendered impotent and, mysteriously, those who have been caught up in his work on the cross have now been brought to "glory," the exact counterpart to shame.

Shame and Golgotha

This survey of some of the Gospel accounts together with the later reflections of the New Testament writers has illustrated that, far from being a peripheral motif in the biblical drama, encountering shame is central to an interpretation of the life and ministry of Jesus. The many different encounters between Jesus and the ordinary people of his day constantly emphasize his search for shamed people, to set free those imprisoned by it, to release the oppressed and to proclaim the year of the Lord's favor. If the life of Jesus was characterized by his willingness to enter into the places that the most shamed inhabit, then we must expect that the final days of his life on earth would simply continue that pattern.

During the period of Roman supremacy and imperial might, crucifixion became known as the *summum supplicium*—the ultimate punishment.[12] It was generally reserved for slaves and those considered to be at the bottom of the social pecking order and was intended to be a powerful political deterrent. Hengel describes its potency: "by the public display of a naked victim at a prominent place—at a crossroads, in the theater, on high ground, at the place of his crime—crucifixion represented the uttermost humiliation, which had a numinous dimension to it."[13] The location of Christ's death—Golgotha, a place outside the walls of the city—fits this pattern perfectly. It was a deeply symbolic place, a place for those who do not belong to society, the unwanted, the scum of the earth. Furthermore, his crucifixion exposed Christ in his *nakedness*. His clothing had been removed and became the object of desire, a trophy for those who had been complicit in his death. To be naked had become over the centuries a deeply shameful thing. The innocent nakedness of Adam and Eve had been replaced with shameful nakedness, as we see so vividly recorded in the story of Noah and his sons in Gen 9:20–27. Crucifixion was a form of death reserved by the Romans only for those who were considered beneath contempt. If the intent of execution was to inflict torture then it would have lasted over a period of days, during which every ounce of terror and pain was extracted. Death through crucifixion was, by comparison, relatively swift for the weight of the body upon the diaphragm would have caused asphyxiation. Part of the intent of crucifixion was to heap *shame* on the victim to an ultimate extent and as such was reserved only for slaves and those who were not Roman citizens. In the culture of the time there could have been no more perfect way in which to shame someone. The experience of the crucifixion was intentionally a public spectacle, intended to cause maximum humiliation and disgrace, such that Paul was able to later refer to this by quoting the Deuteronomic text, "cursed is everyone who hangs upon a tree" (Gal 3:13 quoting Deut 21:23). At each stage of

12. Hengel, *Crucifixion*, 33.

13. Ibid., 87.

his arrest, trial, and execution Jesus is ritually, intentionally, and sadistically shamed, and with each succeeding humiliating incident he absorbs it and inverts its meaning. The narrators of the Gospel accounts of the crucifixion invite readers to notice how, even at such a moment of extremity, Jesus is able to honor his mother by providing for her by asking the beloved disciple to care for her. Throughout the torturous process Jesus is paradoxically presented as both a victim of events but also in control of those same events. He knows when his task is completed, so that he is able to utter the cry, "It is finished!" His death on the cross was the product of powerful political and spiritual forces ranged against him yet he chose freely to enter that place of shame. The decision was entirely his and in so doing he displayed a dignity that could never finally be removed from him. Shame is turned repeatedly into honor and this is how he "shamed shame" for us. The combination of shaming events is presented by the Gospel writers to illustrate the depths to which Christ was shamed on our behalf. In so doing Christ's actions draw a deep resonance from deep within all those who have ever entered into their own shamed condition.

That personal journey of exploration is, for many, almost too painful and dark to endure. Shame resides in that primal, existential part of us that is unutterable in its intensity. It express itself at times in the simple but tortured cry from the heart: Not good enough! It is the experience of sensing that we are not good enough to merit the exuberant grace of God and that maybe we are also not good enough to simply belong to human society and find a place of dignity. It is a truly desperate disease of the soul. If the atonement is only framed in judicial terms, with a declaration of "innocence" being pronounced upon those who put their trust in Christ, then I fear that the intensity of the shame experience will remain untouched. If the story of Jesus is retold, however, in terms of the one who deliberately, intentionally, purposefully seeks out all those who have been shamed—as well as those who have been the instigators of shame—then the narrative takes on a far deeper, more personal, more transforming hue. It is this Christ who not only understands our shamed condition but who has himself entered into the depths of shame for us. He has lowered himself down to the bottom of that poisoned well and drunk it dry.

11

Face

It is time now to return to the theme of the face, which was introduced to us in the opening chapters of the Bible. If shame results in a turning away from the face (*pānîm*) of God and indeed from the faces of others, then it would be unsurprising to find that the redemption and healing of shame is likewise linked to the face of God. In the experience of shame, the intensity of the experience is always recorded visually, on the face of the one who has been shamed. It is our faces that announce who we are, that provide us with an identity, and indeed tell the story of our lives. Our faces declare our humanity. This is captured most eloquently in this poem titled "From Failure Up" by Patrick Kavanagh:[1]

> Can a man grow from the dead clod of failure
> Some consoling flower
> Something humble as a dandelion or a daisy,
> Something to wear as a buttonhole in Heaven?
> Under that flat, flat grief of defeat maybe
> Hope is a seed.
> Maybe this is what he was born for, this hour
> Of hopelessness.
> Maybe it is here he must search
> In this hell of unfaith

1. http://www.augustinians.ie/galway/newsletter/2003/MSG-02-02-03.htm.

Where no one has a purpose
Where the web of Meaning is broken threads
And one man looks at another in fear.
O God can a man find You when he lies with his face downwards
And his nose in the rubble that was his achievements?
Is the music playing behind the door of despair?
O God give us purpose.

One of the most remarkable statements in recent years about guilt, shame, and their connection with "the face" came from President George Bush in the immediate aftermath of the September 11th attacks. "Freedom itself was attacked this morning by a faceless coward," he declared, "and freedom will be defended. Make no mistake, the United States will hunt down and punish those responsible for these cowardly acts."[2] What Bush was doing was dehumanizing and indeed demonizing the enemy who had attacked America by asserting that those people who commit such shameful atrocities did not possess a face. Without a face, they could be hunted down and eliminated. In human terms the face is the most expressive part of the body. Anyone who has engaged in or observed the process of breastfeeding will have noticed how the infant will stare into the face of the mother. This gaze is more than just idle curiosity. The infant is "reading" the face of the mother, and is looking for the experience of being unconditionally loved and affirmed. The period of breastfeeding is now acknowledged to be crucial in the process of bonding and identity formation and it is the gaze that is exchanged between mother and child that is at the heart of the relationship. The influential theory of attachment put forward by the psychologist John Bowlby places bonding or attachment at the core of what it means to be a healthy human being. It is the early bonding, the bonding that takes place when an infant and a parent exchange their loving gaze, that is so fundamental to the later development of a healthy self-concept. Bowlby's theory is nothing more than that which is affirmed repeatedly in the pages of Scripture where wholeness and security are depicted using the language of face. One of the richest sources of such language is found in the Psalms. Here is a selection.

Ps 34:5 "Those who look to him are radiant, their faces are never covered with shame."

2. http://www.americanrhetoric.com/speeches/gwbush911barksdale.html.

Ps 67:1 "May God be gracious to us and bless us and make his face shine upon us, that your ways may be known on earth, your salvation among all nations."

Ps 80:3 "Restore us, O God Almighty; make your face shine upon us, that we may be saved."

There is a simple pattern presented here. The experience of knowing the face of God gazing upon us is nothing other than the experience of salvation itself; the two belong together. It is by looking into the face of God that the Psalmist finds salvation and it is in the converse of this, the hiding of God's face, that divine abandonment is experienced, resulting in shame. Jacob found that this was precisely the result of his experience of wrestling with God described for us in Gen 32. At the conclusion of a tortuous tale of betrayal and intrigue, Jacob meets his estranged brother Esau. The anticipation of that reunion heightens the tension such that Jacob hopes to pacify his brother with lavish gifts so that eventually he may see him face to face. In one single verse—Gen 32:20—the word "face" (*pānîm*) is used four times denoting the profound significance of this encounter. It was to be a defining moment in which the two brothers would see each other's faces and thereby be reconciled. Yet Jacob's adventure continues into the night. He receives a divine visitor with whom he struggles until he receives the blessing that he craves. This blessing would be the seal of God's approval and acceptance of Jacob after a lifetime of less than honorable living. Eventually the struggle is concluded and Jacob knows that this was a truly powerful, pivotal meeting with God. How does he describe such an intense encounter? From the lips of Jacob, these words are uttered: "I saw God face to face." The intensity of that moment was both deeply humbling yet also profoundly healing and Jacob was not the same person after his encounter with the face of God. His name was changed to Israel, the name of the nation that would be descended from him, and the venue of the wrestling match was called *Pĕnî'ēl*, meaning "the face of God." It is surely of the most critical significance that God's chosen people are named after the man who experienced a *face-to-face* encounter with the living God.

The prophet Isaiah articulates the significance of the face when the issue of shame is being faced. The passage in chapter 50 which describes the Servant of Yahweh, a text which has obvious christological resonances (Matt 27:30–31), states:

> The Sovereign LORD has opened my ears, and I have not been rebellious; I have not drawn back. I offered my back to those who beat me, my cheeks to those who pulled out my beard; I did not hide my face from mocking and spitting. Because the Sovereign LORD helps me, I will not be disgraced. Therefore have I set my face like flint, and I know I will not be put to shame. He who vindicates me is near. Who then will bring charges against me? Let us face each other! Who is my accuser? Let him confront me! It is the Sovereign LORD who helps me. Who is he who will condemn me?

Here the Servant of the Lord knows that he is innocent, he has not been rebellious or stubborn. He has willingly allowed himself to be shamed by having his beard pulled and being spat at in public. These are forms of public humiliation yet the Servant sets his face "like flint," presumably facing towards the Sovereign Lord who helps him. In turning his face towards the face of God, there is no shame, but only vindication. There is no condemnation but only liberty from the false accusations of those who circle around him.

When Christ cries out, "My God, my God, why have you forsaken me?" we see him in the agony of divine abandonment. This desperate prayer formed the tragic counterpart to the voice of his Father at the moment of his baptism. As he emerged from the waters of the Jordan, he heard the voice from heaven affirming him with the words, "You are my Son, whom I love. In you I am well pleased." They were the words that impelled and empowered him throughout his ministry. He knew that, whatever else befell him, he remained the beloved Son of the Father. There could be nothing more existentially vital than the knowledge that this was true. Yet as the final moments of his earthly life drew near, the Father's voice grew fainter, until it appeared that it had been silenced forever. The pain of divine abandonment was the lowest point of the entire episode. The mocking and humiliation from those present was dreadful and intensely painful; yet the experience of the utter abandonment by his Father was worse. It signaled the final expulsion from the trinitarian embrace, the ultimate separation from the community of grace to which he belonged. It was the declaration that he was now alone, discarded, abandoned, forsaken, in the place of shame together with everyone else who had ever inhabited that place.

His agonized utterance, drawn from Ps 22, suggests that his experience of abandonment is directly related to the sense of loss of the gaze of the Father. Later in that same psalm there is the hope that one day the Psalmist will be restored from his place of affliction. That restoration will occur when the hidden face of God is turned once more towards those he loves. "For he has not despised or scorned the suffering of the afflicted one; he has not hidden his face from him but has listened to his cry for help" (Ps 22:24). At last, Jesus on the cross breathes his last and utters the cry, "Into your hands I commit my Spirit." It is a line taken from Ps 31, a Psalm that is full of references to God's face and its resonance with the removal of shame.

> In you, O LORD, I have taken refuge; let me never be put to shame; deliver me in your righteousness . . . Into your hands I commit my spirit; redeem me, O LORD, the God of truth . . . My life is consumed by anguish and my years by groaning; my strength fails because of my affliction, and my bones grow weak. Because of all my enemies, I am the utter contempt of my neighbors; I am a dread to my friends—those who see me on the street flee from me. I am forgotten by them as though I were dead; I have become like broken pottery. For I hear the slander of many; there is terror on every side; they conspire against me and plot to take my life. But I trust in you, O LORD; I say, You are my God . . . Let your face shine on your servant; save me in your unfailing love. Let me not be put to shame, O LORD, for I have cried out to you; but let the wicked be put to shame and lie silent in the grave.

At the epicenter of the event of the cross, we witness Christ's engagement with shame in all its terror and his constant endeavor to feel the face of his Father resting upon him. It is when this face appears to be turned away that the suffering of Christ becomes most acute. On his face, at that moment, we see the cost of God's initiative in bodily form. It is a human face that is in torment, the face of one who is in a place of shame. It is the same human face of Christ that had continually made a loving appeal to all with whom there had been an encounter. It is the face of Jesus that records the intensity of his compassion as he stands above the city and weeps over Jerusalem. That same face is filled with tears as he approaches the grave of his beloved friend Lazarus. It is the face that looked at Peter after his threefold denial. In that one glance Peter knew that his weakness had been exposed and judged by Christ. His feeling of shame at that moment was acute; his tears were bitter. Yet in that look upon the face of the condemned Christ, Peter also knew that the exposure of his sin was tempered with grace. But perhaps the most powerful instance of the transforming face of Christ is seen at the moment of his transfiguration. The story informs us that Jesus takes three disciples with him up a mountain to pray. While on the mountain the group is enveloped in the glory of God. Luke describes what happens next. "As he was praying, the appearance of his face changed, and his clothes became as bright as a flash of lightning" (Luke 9:29). As the three disciples gaze upon the transfigured face of Christ they hear the voice of the Father urging them to listen to everything the Son has to say. It is as if the face of Christ draws them magnetically, and in that gaze they are consumed with awe. Clarke has beautifully encapsulated the quality of that moment. "The Father's voice calls out to the worshippers in an unashamed gaze upon the Son, words that reflect a face turned towards the Son in love."[3]

Soon after this incident, at a pivotal time in his ministry, Christ "sets his face" towards Jerusalem for the time had come to trigger the final stage of his entire mission. His decision to face the political and religious powers of his day would inevitably lead to his death, and on that first Good Friday we are confronted with not only the agonized, tormented face of Christ, but also with the dead face. That is the end of this particular chapter of his task, the apparent failure, the triumph of the powers of evil over him, a corpse on a cross with eyes closed. How can such a gruesome image become a place of healing and restoration? It is a question that demands an answer, given that all of the preceding discussion has presumed that a dialogue between God's face and ours is not only possible but existentially critical. How is it possible, therefore, for an exchange to take place, for communication to happen between humanity and the dead face of the crucified Christ? Can a dead face speak?

Interpreting "Face"

We can approach this question in a variety of ways. One of these is by way of mourning. The face of a dead person indicates the finality of a life. This life has come to an end and now is the time to recognize that loss and to enter into a period of healing grief. It is not uncommon in some cultures to use an open coffin so that mourners can gaze upon the face of the deceased as an integral part of their farewell. The pain of those who

3. Clarke, "We Live before the Faces of Others," 33.

have lost loved ones through a tragedy that deprives the family of a body compounds their anguish. How can mourning occur if there is no dead face to gaze upon? One is left in a state of limbo, suspended, waiting, hoping, longing, but unable to move on. The face of the dead, whilst tragic because it signifies loss, is ultimately freeing for it communicates that a period of time has passed, a life has been lived and it is time to move forward. The dead face of Christ achieved precisely this result. It signified the utter finality and totality of his self-giving. All of his life was given for the sake of others and his death was the outcome of that trajectory, the natural consequence of his path of self-donation. Joseph of Aramathea and the two Marys summoned the courage to identify themselves with this dead body and took upon themselves the task of giving the dead Jesus an appropriate, dignified burial. For Joseph it was a moment of disclosure. Here was a man, a member of the council, associated with the religious powers of his day, choosing to make plain his discipleship of the shamed and humiliated carpenter from Nazareth. It was the dead face of Christ that galvanized him into action.

Not only is the dead face of a loved one an occasion for the outpouring of grief, but it may also become powerfully symbolic. Images of the assassinated Martin Luther King lying in his coffin provided such an iconic image that empowered and strengthened a generation to continue his struggle. The "voice" of his dead face spoke loudly. In like manner, the iconoclastic controversy of the eight and ninth centuries, which engendered so much heat, turned around the question of the power of the portrayal of the dead face of Christ. "For the Christian world from that moment on," wrote Marie-Jose Baudinet, "the theology of the face is the key to power."[4]

Another avenue of exploration concerns the handing over of responsibility. What happens to those left behind when the face is no longer there? In the garden of Gethsemane, Jesus turned away from his disciples to be alone with the Father for a while. Yet in that turning away the disciples were challenged to accompany him in prayer during the hour of his greatest need. The absence of his face before them marked the moment when their responsibility began. In similar fashion the sleeping face of Christ in the bottom of a boat during a storm did not mean that no communication was taking place. On the contrary, Christ's unconscious face

4. Ford, *Self and Salvation*, 207.

spoke of his trust that, through faith, they were able to endure the storm and not give way to fear. The fact that in both stories the disciples failed to read the signs of the absent or sleeping face of Christ demonstrated that they were yet to learn how his face possesses the power to communicate in whatever form it is manifested.

A further way of addressing that question is to approach it by way of empathy. The capacity to empathize is the ability to imagine oneself in the place of another, to feel what the other feels and thereby to come alongside in true compassion. Empathy is the deliberate action of setting aside one's own agenda and needs and staying, for a while at least, in the place of someone else in imaginative participation in his or her suffering. Empathy demands the highest degree of creativity and listening. In one sense that is exactly what Jesus came to achieve: To enter into the most shameful places that humans inhabit and to feel for himself the devastating consequences of that shame. Unavoidably, shame is writ large on our own faces for it cannot be easily hidden or concealed. On the cross, the human Christ entered completely into the darkest places of shame, feeling the full force of that estrangement.

Finally, the dead face of Christ speaks of sacrifice. We have already explored how the sacrificial system functioned, being the means of offering to God something costly in place of another. Jesus was fully aware that by submitting to the human powers that be, he would be executed for political and religious reasons. The human instrumentation of his death did not detract from his willing participation in it. He chose to become a sacrifice and all those familiar with the sacrificial system knew that a sacrifice only became effective when the lifeblood was poured out. His dead face spoke of this final outpouring. The sacrifice was completed and accomplished and announced by the lifelessness of his face.

The cry of dereliction uttered by Christ on the cross marked the final accomplishment of his mission. He had come to seek and to save the lost, to look out for those who had been excluded from society, whose existence had been called into question, whose intrinsic worth had been denied. Their experience of lostness was to be shut out from relational engagement, to be denied the life-giving exchange that occurs when the individual "I" meets the "you" of another person. That I–You encounter ultimately derives its significance from the originating I–You that occurs between God and humanity. Jesus lived before the face of his Father throughout his life and that bond of love between the Father and the Son, sealed through the work of the Holy Spirit, was the foundation of his entire sense of being and purpose. At the final moment on the cross when he felt the full force of the shameful estrangement, the bond was broken, or at least in the experience of the dying Christ that is how it *felt*. For Christ to feel the loss of the loving gaze of his Father signified his full entry into the experience of shame, to be consumed by terror of God's abandonment, his face obscured, his love quenched.

Shame, Face, and the Resurrection

The four Gospels offer us a surprisingly mundane account of the resurrection appearances. There are no trumpets or hosts of angels, no transcendent radiance, no sense of triumphalism. It is all very ordinary in one sense, yet with some extraordinary twists. In all the differing accounts there is a disturbance in the ability of the disciples to recognize Jesus. In the well-known story of the Emmaus Road, Luke records that the traveling companions of the risen Jesus were "kept from recognizing him." Their non-recognition of Jesus in the first part of the Emmaus narrative meant that the resurrection story held no intrinsic power and effected no change within them despite the burning of the hearts within as he explained the Scriptures. It was only at the point of *recognition*, when the bread was broken, that a change occurred and the mystery was unlocked. The crucial moment was the sudden God-given ability to look on the face of their unbidden guest and to see there the face of the resurrected Christ. Without this facial recognition, the resurrection was an event without meaning.

Amongst the four Gospels, John's account appears to place the greatest emphasis on gazing upon the face of Christ as the means by which salvation is effected. During his conversation with Nicodemus at night, Jesus explains that just as Moses lifted up the bronze snake in the wilderness and all those who raised their eyes towards it were healed, so must he be lifted up (John 3:14). All those who gaze upon the uplifted face of the Christ will likewise enjoy healing. The healing comes through the gaze, a faithful and faith-filled gaze upon Christ. John returns to this theme in the final chapter of his Gospel, where Jesus appears on the beach, yet the disciples "did not realize that it was him" (John 21:4). As soon as they recognized his face the scene is transformed from a peaceful tale of some early morning fishermen to the explosive story of an engagement with the risen Christ. But perhaps the most poignant of all the resurrection accounts is found in John 20 where Jesus appears to the frightened disciples huddled behind locked doors. He stands before them and speaks words of peace repeatedly while breathing the gift of the Holy Spirit upon their uplifted faces. This face-to-face encounter mirrors the story of God breathing into Adam in Gen 2. Both stories depict the divine-human encounter in the most intimate of terms—standing facing one another with the breath of the divine being given to humankind. It is this kind of encounter that is so profoundly restoring and healing. David Ford writes movingly about our facing towards the risen Christ: "The risen face of Jesus is a 'revelation' not in the sense of making him plain in a straightforward manner. Rather what is 'unveiled' is a face that transcends simple recognisability, that eludes our categories, and stretches our capacities in the way in which God does. It provokes fear, bewilderment, doubt, joy, and amazement. It therefore is profoundly questioning and questionable. It generates a community whose life before this face is endlessly interrogative and whose response to it leads into ever new complexities, ambiguities, joys. and sufferings."[5]

Not only does John appear to place an emphasis on gazing upwards and towards the uplifted Christ but there is also another thread running through his Gospel. It is the theme of *glory*. John is not alone in mentioning glory, but of the four Gospel writers he gives it the greatest weight. Glory is first introduced to us in the biblical account in the book of Exodus where the Hebrew word *kābēd* carried the sense of weight or heaviness. It denoted an experience of profound and awesome mystery, indicative of being in the presence of someone of great dignity and worth. If the glory of God descended, as in Isaiah's vision (Isa 6), the only appropriate response was to bow down in adoration. In the New Testament glory (*doxa*) carries a slightly different connotation, one of exultant praise and thanksgiving, and it is from this Greek root that we derive our word "doxology." In both cases, glory is naturally paired with honor, the exact counterpart to shame.

John's record of Christ's lengthy prayer in John 17 is full of references to glory. Christ begins his prayer with, "And now, Father, glorify me in your presence with the glory I had with you before the world be-

5. Ford, *Self and Salvation*, 172.

gan" (v. 5), acknowledging that the kind of relationship that has always existed between the Father and the Son is "glorious," filled with weighty awesomeness and joyful praise. This glory, the possession of the Son, is now to be given to all those who place their trust in him: "I have given them the glory that you gave me, that they may be one as we are one" (v. 22). John's intention is thus to explain how the glory that is intrinsic to the very being of God is his gift to us now. Paul too takes up this theme and connects the resurrection of Christ with the gift of glory. In his extended discussion on the historicity and the meaning of the resurrection in 1 Cor 15, he pens these words: "So will it be with the resurrection of the dead. The body that is sown is perishable, it is raised imperishable; it is sown in dishonor, it is raised in glory; it is sown in weakness, it is raised in power" (1 Cor 15:42–43). Paul here is making a startling contrast between the state of our physical bodies and the powerful healing effect of the resurrection of Christ. Two words are placed in opposition to each other—dishonor and glory. The Greek word translated here as "dishonor" is *atimia*, a word that elsewhere is rendered as "shame" (e.g., 1 Cor 11:14). This *atimia*, which is the tragic depiction of the condition of humankind, is replaced with "glory"—*doxa*. Paul's mature theological reflections on the nature of the resurrection lead him to the conclusion that the meaning of this extraordinary event is that *shame* is replaced with *glory and honor*. The resurrected Christ, upon whom we are invited to gaze, offers us the prospect of our shame being removed and in its place the gift of honor and glory is bestowed. The answer to the agonized question that Christ addressed to his Father on the cross comes on Easter Sunday with the appearing of the face of Jesus. This risen Christ brings honor to those who gaze upon his face.

It is surely not insignificant that the church at Corinth, which had turned in upon itself in shame, was called to look upon the face of Christ. This is the theme of 2 Cor 3 where Paul contrasts the glory of the new covenant with the glory of the covenant given at Sinai. Paul's argument is that the covenant given then possessed a glory that was written all over the face of Moses. Yet the new covenant is greater than this and has a transforming dynamic effect. "And all of us, with unveiled faces, seeing the glory of the Lord as though reflected in a mirror, are being transformed into the same image from one degree of glory to another; for this comes from the Lord, the Spirit" (2 Cor 3:18). David Ford in commenting on this text writes, "This key text illuminates a double correlation between a community beholding the face of God and itself being transformed, and then in turn experiencing a transformation in the way it faces the world. The Christian church itself, burdened indeed by a terrible story over the centuries of being instrumental in the quest for power, wealth, and coercion, must face the Face of the one that embraces suffering on the cross."[6]

Gazing upon the face of the crucified and risen Christ became an enduring and empowering metaphor for the early church. We witness this in the opening verses of the book of Revelation, a text written to encourage a suffering and persecuted Christian community struggling to survive in the face of the overwhelming might of the Roman Empire. It contains vivid apocalyptic literature, intended to encourage the growth of confident, free, new communities of God's redeemed people. From where will these communities derive their identity? What will give them a sense of honor and purpose? How will they become confident and bold? From gazing upon the form of the risen Christ who is described as having a face "like the sun shining in full strength" (Rev 1:16). The final consummation of the work of Christ is depicted in images that tumble over one another as the writer attempts to point the reader towards a heavenly reality. In that place of perfection, "the throne of God and the Lamb shall be in it and his servants shall worship him; they shall see his face and his name shall be on their foreheads" (Rev. 22:3–4). The healing experience of looking at the face of Christ is intensely personal, corporate, and relational. Christ enters the "space" of humanity but this does not happen at humanity's expense. There is no competition between God's space and ours. Indeed we are invited into the freedom of "face-to-face" partnership with God, which leads not to our extinction or humiliation but to our liberation and to honor.

If the appearing of the face of God was the ultimate experience of blessing under the old covenant—expressed so powerfully in the Aaronic blessing (Num 6:22–26)—and the recognition of the risen face of Christ effected a similar response of being caught up in the mystery of God's redeeming work, then an urgent question begs to be addressed. To what human condition or predicament does the divine face offer healing and redemption? We may answer, albeit somewhat glibly, that it addresses the question of human sinfulness, but such a response does not really satisfy,

6. Ibid., 200.

for sin is a many-headed beast distorting and misshaping our world. If sin is solely construed in terms of our guilty status before God then the language of "face" has no genuine resonance. Guilt is a legal term and transgressions of the law require a legal remedy and there is no question that the Bible uses legal language at times, as we have already noted. Yet the category of "face" does not belong in the law court. To gaze upon the face of someone else is essentially an *intimate* act. It is an action that reaches towards another, desiring to know, to understand, to appreciate, to give respect, to forgive. The appearing of the divine face turned towards humankind is best paired with the deeply personal yet profoundly political experience of shame. It is precisely at the point of the gaze that the language of exchange becomes profoundly appropriate. We have already explored how such language can appear cold, calculating, mathematical; doing nothing to touch the deepest recesses of the human heart. If exchange language is used in such a way, then the atonement can be reduced to a formula describing an event that is outside of us, yet somehow is about us. The language of exchange in the context of a gaze is of an entirely different order. It has nothing to do with symmetry or mutuality or equivalence or the balancing of books. It is far more intimate than any of these. The exchange of glances between lovers is a metaphor that is closer to the mark, or the exchange of looks between mother and infant. Such exchanges speak to the soul and tell a story of unconditional acceptance, thorough-knowing, complete oneness, perfect love. Such exchanges can only heal, restore, and empower.

The mutuality of Christ gazing upon us in love and us reciprocating that gaze is an image of redemption and restoration. The face of Christ conveys a depth of interaction with humanity that calls for a response of thanksgiving and praise. It deals with the loss of respect and value that all of humanity feels. It treats the experience and condition of shame with the utmost seriousness, yet counts it as nothing and replaces it with honor. The apostle Paul alludes to this in his Letter to the Romans. At the beginning of chapter 5 he writes about the peace with God that has been accomplished through the work of Christ and then he goes on to speak of hope in the midst of suffering. "We also rejoice in our sufferings, because we know that suffering produces perseverance, perseverance, character; and character, hope. And hope does not disappoint us, because God has poured out his love into our hearts by the Holy Spirit, whom he has given us" (Rom 5:3–5).

The phrase translated here in the New International Version as "and hope does not disappoint us," does not properly bring out the sense of the original Greek where the word *kataischunō* is used. This compound word is derived from *aischunomai*, which means to feel or experience shame. What Paul is saying therefore is that the end product of the experience of suffering, within the economy of God, is hope. This hope is mysterious in that it is not grounded in something visible or tangible but is simply a result of the gift of the Spirit. While this hope might appear to others to be foolish or ill-founded, in reality this hope does not bring us into a place of shame. The fact that hope is paired in opposition to shame is highly significant. The fledgling Christian community confounded its critics by displaying a resilient hope in the midst of great suffering and tragedy, yet this foolish hope did not bring those early Christians into shame, but rather into an experience of glory. Perhaps the final word on the power of the resurrected Christ to replace shame with glory should remain therefore with the apostle Paul: "For God, who said, 'Let light shine out of darkness,' made his light shine in our hearts to give us the light of the knowledge of the glory of God in the face of Christ" (2 Cor 4:6).

12

Stories

MAKING SENSE OF THE big story is a demanding task. One has to join up
the dots of the smaller stories in such a way as to treat each story with
the greatest integrity and to know how each one is related to the others.
The final picture that is drawn has many facets, differing hues, and subtle
nuances. It would be a pity to take these astounding stories and reduce
them by a process of theological distillation to a set of systematic doctri-
nal propositions. An alternative way to bring this study to a conclusion is
to finish in the same way that the investigation began—with stories. So I
offer four stories which attempt to bring together some of the themes we
have so far explored, each with a slightly different emphasis.

- *Leaving the Turtle Shell* is an autobiographical account of the experience of one woman who had suffered the most acute shame and yet,
  through the action of the Holy Spirit at work within her and in others, is brought to a place of wholeness.

- *The Thanksgiving Liturgy* portrays the story of Christ's reconciling
  love within the context of a Eucharistic prayer.

- *A Healing Liturgy for the Shamed* offers a liturgical structure for a
  healing service for those who have been shamed.

- *The Heartbeat* traces the story of the entire Bible in 750 words. Its central theme is the heartbeat of the love of God, which never diminishes.

Taken together these stories illustrate, I hope, that the healing of shame is both deeply personal and profoundly political. It is private and public. It goes to the heart of who we are as individuals and who we are as nations and communities.

Leaving the Turtle Shell

I am sitting in a corner of a bathroom, anxiously watching the door. I press my body against the wall. I wish I could merge with the wall and become invisible. I am freezing.

Then, prompted again, my memory revealed another picture. I was pushed around, first against a wall, and then onto the bed. I could not hold this memory. It was too painful. For a moment everything around me went black—but to my relief I "woke up" in the present, sitting in a light room, in safety. We gave it another try. This time I remembered my intense fear of becoming pregnant. I remembered trying to stop Richard who seemed totally out of control; the hungry look on his face and my immense helplessness and fear. Sarah, my counselor, understood. "He raped you, didn't he?" she simply stated. It was like a shock. These words stayed with me for many weeks—as if I could hear her saying them again and again. Rape. Such a horrible word. Impossible to pronounce it myself. Was that really rape? Isn't this something that only occurs in late night films and criminal novels—but not in real life? Richard had not been hiding behind a bush in a park after dark, it had happened in my own flat. So wasn't it my fault after all?

Bringing this memory to the surface was like opening Pandora's Box. This incident had just been the last one of countless others. More memories, deeper and darker ones, emerged. I found myself in a sea of feelings of horror and confusion. Words did not reach there. I was thrown back to the infant stage, or what I imagine it to be—life in a sensory world, without logic or patterns, no language or coherent stories, just pictures. The memories came over me at any time of the day or the night.

I am lying on my bed, face down. I cannot move. He is lying on top of me—I feel the heavy weight of his body. His weight compresses my chest. My face is buried in a pillow, I cannot see anything and I don't want to. I can hardly breathe either. As I struggle to get free, he exerts pressure on my head, holds me down. I desperately try to inhale, but I can't get any air into my lungs. I seem to be inhaling fabric. I start to panic and to fight; hot flashes run through my body. I need air now! The fighting seems to excite him; he pushes even harder. Doesn't he understand that this is not a game? I fight with all my strength, which grows in parallel to my desperation. My arms try to push him away, my legs kick. In the end, I succeed. I manage to turn my head to the side and to get my face out of the pillow. AIR! It is wonderful to fill my lungs with air, wonderful beyond description. The adrenaline rush abates; I am totally exhausted. To him, this has just been foreplay, and things take their usual course. I don't have the strength to fight him any longer. At the moment, I am content with being alive.

Very often, my body remembered incidents before my mind did. Pain in my lungs told me about suffocation, pain in my wrists about my arms being tied together, and pain in my back reminded me of being beaten. These "sensory memories" sometimes troubled me for weeks before the complete stories emerged in my mind. At first, I clung to the possibility that these memories might not be real, that they were nothing but bad dreams. Denial was a well-proven strategy: throughout that relationship I had done my best to pretend that everything was "normal," "not so serious," that we had had "just a silly little argument." I had been quite successful in convincing myself and others—nobody seemed to notice anything unusual. Only once did a friendly neighbor make an attempt to talk to me about what was going on in our home. I totally panicked—I was shocked that someone had discovered my dirty secret. My feelings of shame were overwhelming. It never occurred to me that she wanted to help me, not criticize me. I reassured her that everything was fine and fled. From that moment on, I was even more vigilant than before, always wondering if what Richard did to me was somehow visible to people, and what they would think of me "if they only knew."

The situation got worse over time. Like an addict, Richard needed higher and higher doses of sex and violence to get the same satisfaction, and his practices became all the more cruel and bizarre. I had to develop more efficient strategies to distance myself from the abuse I experienced.

I imagined being a turtle. The turtle could hide under a strong shell and nobody could get in there. Richard could only touch the shell. He could do to it whatever he liked, but he would never be able to touch the "real" me. With the thick shell around me, I stopped feeling anything. I was just "gone," waiting for the violence to end, for him to leave, or to fall asleep. Afterwards, I instinctively knew I had to forget if I wanted to survive. Forgetting often happened in a quite literal and almost ritualized way: the "dirty" feeling turned into violent waves of sickness, as if my body wanted to clean itself from the inside. This usually continued until complete exhaustion and some sort of blackout put an end to it.

I want to get myself a glass of water—my stomach is burning, my throat is burning, everything is burning . . . But all I can do is sit down and lean against the wall. Touching the cool tiles with my hot face brings some relief. My heart is pounding rapidly; I am withdrawing into the inside of my body. The room disappears, everything turns black around me, and the only sound I can hear is my own heartbeat. I know that I am falling, falling endlessly into the dark. There is no ground, nothing to stop me. I embrace this merciful darkness that lets me forget the world around me.

When I woke up again, I never seemed to wonder how I had ended up on the bathroom floor. I hurriedly got dressed, cleaned up all traces of the preceding incident, and got on with life. Nothing had happened.

After the first counseling sessions, the flood of painful memories started to break down all barriers of numbness. There was no valve for all these intense feelings, no escape. Sometimes, it was hard to resist destructive impulses. I wanted to run into a wall. Do something that hurts. I wanted to feel "real pain" rather than emotional pain—the sort that can be treated with painkillers. I wanted to get drunk, to forget, if only for a little while. Get a good dose of sleeping pills and sleep without nightmares for once. I don't know how I would have survived this phase if Sarah had not taught me to turn to Jesus whenever I needed to, to picture him close to me, holding my hand. With him at my side I could cope. Sarah also instructed me in slow and rhythmic breathing, which was remarkably effective in dispelling my feelings of panic. If anyone had asked me at that time what I had been doing all day, my honest answer would have been "breathing."

After a while I learned to handle my distress to a degree that would allow me to address the memories. But expressing them also required overcoming the shame that had kept me silent for so long, which was an even bigger challenge. I felt responsible for the sexual violence I had experienced, wondering if I had encouraged Richard in any way, or if I could have resisted more effectively. But interestingly, the question of responsibility, or guilt, was actually of quite limited importance. I felt dirty, damaged, and what had happened could never be undone. What I had experienced was far beyond my wildest imagination. "Normal" people don't even know about these things, I assumed, so, guilty or not, I had lost my place in normal society. My body felt contaminated, affected by a form of "cancer" that had spread everywhere. I wanted to take off my skin, but even that would not have helped—the contamination went deeper, into every cell of my body. It made me feel sad and hopeless knowing that my greatest wishes could never be granted: I so much wanted to be one of those happy and innocent people who have never experienced these perversions of human nature. I so much wanted to have a new body. A clean one.

I think I reached a real turning point in tackling the feelings of shame when Sarah suggested imagining the "dirty" part of me that I so much despised as a separate person. I pictured this person looking like I did during the relationship with Richard: a girl with long hair, quite thin, shy, and afraid. Separated from this "scared" part, the rest of me felt stronger and so much more filled with life. Looking at my "scared" part from the outside, all the feelings of resentment simply disappeared. I felt nothing but pity and the desire to protect this girl that looked so hurt and afraid. Then, in my imagination, I tried to make these two people meet, to imagine the person I am now putting an arm around the person I was then. This required quite some practice—the "scared" girl seemed to hide, she did not trust the more confident person I am today. When I finally managed, I felt great warmth and acceptance. "It's called becoming whole" Sarah said with a smile. And that is exactly how it felt.

Even without this great burden of shame, it took a conscious decision to stop hiding. I still seemed to disappear under my turtle shell all too often when I would actually have preferred to relax and enjoy other people's company. Instead of protecting me, the shell had become my prison. So one evening, this became the subject of my prayer. God seemed to ask me if I was really sure about my request to remove the shell—if I was ready to feel my vulnerability, to just be me, as I am, without disguise. I hesitated for a moment, but then I chose freedom over security and decided that I wanted to leave the shell. As soon as I had made this decision, I could almost feel the shell break. It was a permanent change—the next time I instinctively tried to withdraw under it, I noticed that it simply wasn't there anymore. I had to cope without it.

Despite these wonderful and sometimes frightening experiences of healing, recovery is still an ongoing process. Sometimes new memories make their way to the surface and sometimes old ones come back to haunt me for a while. But every time this happens it gets easier to deal with them. My past will always be a part of my life, but it has lost its power over my present and future.

A Thanksgiving Liturgy for the Bread and Wine

> This is the table of invitation, the table of encounter, the table of
> hope.
> This is the moment when you, Lord, give yourself to us,
> you come close, so close that we can even hear, touch, feel, and
> taste you.
>
> You are the Lord of all creation.
> You are the one who holds the stars in the palm of your hand.
> You are the one who only has to say a word and something new is
> born.
> You are the one who takes delight in all that you have made.
>
> And us? What do we have to offer you in return?
> Our lives are a confusing mixture of
> hope and disappointment,
> love and anger,
> celebration and frustration,
> pride and shame.
> We are wounded, broken, frail people.
>
> When you came as an infant child, you astonished the rich and
> poor alike.
> When you came in the midst of a storm your disciples could
> scarcely believe it was you.
> When you walked through the land you noticed the forgotten, the
> excluded, the lonely, and the widowed.

You sought out the outsiders and brought them in.
You spoke to those who were considered as refuse, and in those
     encounters they found honor.

Towards the end of your time on earth, you invited your friends
to share a meal with you and you amazed everyone by kneeling
before them and washing their feet. When the meal was nearly
over you broke bread and poured out wine. You shared these
amongst those present, saying, "Take, eat and drink for when you
do this not only will you remember me, but I will come to you
again and draw close."

So here, in this place, in this way, we recognize your willingness
to come where we are, to suffer in our place, to go to those dark,
deathly places from which we recoil. On the cross you absorbed
in your body our pain, our losses, our sickness, our stubborn
rebelliousness, our disgrace. You look at the shame that we carry
and count it as nothing. And when you rose again, you took us
with you, back to where we truly belong—our true home—as beloved, forgiven, cherished children of God. So thank you. Thank
you that in you we can see the pain and the cost of loving. Thank
you that you still wait for us to hear your insistent call. And in our
hearts we echo that call, crying,

Holy, holy, holy is the Lord.

As we eat this broken bread and drink this wine outpoured, send
your Holy Spirit once more so that we might have eyes to see,
hands to hold, ears to hear, and hearts to treasure your coming to
us again and again and again.

Take this bread, for in so doing, you share in Christ's life and his
     joy.
Drink this wine. It is Christ's own lifeblood poured out to make
     you whole.

A Healing Liturgy for the Shamed

Leader:
You have searched me, LORD, and you know me. You know when I sit and
when I rise; you perceive my thoughts from afar. You discern my going

out and my lying down; you are familiar with all my ways. Before a word is on my tongue you, LORD, know it completely. You hem me in behind and before, and you lay your hand upon me. Such knowledge is too wonderful for me, too lofty for me to attain. Where can I go from your Spirit? Where can I flee from your presence? If I go up to the heavens, you are there; if I make my bed in the depths, you are there. If I rise on the wings of the dawn, if I settle on the far side of the sea, even there your hand will guide me, your right hand will hold me fast. If I say, "Surely the darkness will hide me and the light become night around me," even the darkness will not be dark to you; the night will shine like the day, for darkness is as light to you. For you created my inmost being; you knit me together in my mother's womb. I praise you because I am fearfully and wonderfully made; your works are wonderful, I know that full well. My frame was not hidden from you when I was made in the secret place. When I was woven together in the depths of the earth, your eyes saw my unformed body. All the days ordained for me were written in your book before one of them came to be. How precious to me are your thoughts, are God! How vast is the sum of them! Were I to count them, they would outnumber the grains of sand—when I awake, I am still with you.
(Ps 139:1–18)

> *Congregation: Chant:*
> *O Lord hear my prayer, O Lord hear my prayer, when I call answer me*
> *O Lord hear my prayer, O Lord hear my prayer, come and listen to me.*

Leader:
A bruised reed he will not break,
and a smoldering wick he will not snuff out.
In faithfulness he will bring forth justice.

[Those participating are given a piece of charcoal to hold]

Leader:
Gentle God, we come to you bearing the wounds of our shame.
These wounds have polluted and damaged;
they have dirtied and distorted.

I live in disgrace all day long, and my face is covered with shame.

A bruised reed he will not break,
and a smoldering wick he will not snuff out.
In faithfulness he will bring forth justice.

> *Congregation: Chant*
> *O Lord hear my prayer . . .*

Leader:
Gentle God, you see our scorn, disgrace, and shame.
Words can barely begin to describe what lies within.

Hiding, covering, blaming, raging.
Unclean, unaccepted, unacceptable, unacknowledged.
Dark, alive, sinister, dead.
Coiling, wreathing, wrapping, entangling.
Heavy, loaded, broken, burdened.
Poison, decay, rotten, stinking.
Alone, secret, stored, cellar.
Silent, screaming, sobbing, dying.
Here, now, then, always.

[Space is given for the participant to add his or her own words/images/
feelings]

A bruised reed he will not break,
and a smoldering wick he will not snuff out.
In faithfulness he will bring forth justice.

> *Congregation: Chant*
> *O Lord hear my prayer . . .*

Leader:
Let us fix our eyes on Jesus, the pioneer and perfecter of faith. For the joy
set before him he endured the cross, scorning its shame, and sat down at
the right hand of the throne of God.

[Those participating are invited to lay their piece of charcoal to one side and wash their hands in the water provided]

[Silence]

Leader:

How can we stand before the mirror of God's face, from which nothing can be hidden?

[Each person is invited to take a small mirror and to look at it]

Leader:

You have searched me, LORD, and you know me.
You know when I sit and when I rise;
you perceive my thoughts from afar.

[Silence]

Leader:

Let us hear the voice of the Lord spoken to us.

The LORD bless you and keep you;
The LORD make his face shine on you and be gracious to you;
The LORD turn his face toward you and give you peace.

The LORD kneel before you and protect you from all harm;
The LORD make his face shine on you and show you favor, grace, and
   elegance.
The LORD turn his face toward you and give you complete wholeness.

[Silence]

[Anointing with oil]

Leader:

Receive this anointing and as you do so, may you be given:
a crown of beauty instead of ashes,

the oil of joy instead of mourning,
and a garment of praise
instead of a spirit of despair.

[Blessing]

In the name of the Father who adores you and runs to embrace you;
In the name of the Son who comes looking for you and gives himself for
you;
In the name of the Holy Spirit, the dove, the counselor who is ever beside
you.

Amen.

The Heartbeat

At the heart of all creation there is a heartbeat:

Bmm . . . bmm . . . bmm . . . bmm.

At times the beat quickens, during moments of high anticipation, but then
it returns to its steady rhythm, without pause, without hesitation, day after
day, year after year, unending. It is the pulsing lifeblood of love flowing
from the heart of God towards all that he has made. One day this God will
visit his creation in person. He himself will go and participate in the life of
humanity. He will laugh and cry, encourage and admonish, educate and
confuse, suffer and die, and rise again to the surprise, delight and dismay
of the people with whom he lived. But this is to rush ahead to the end of
the story.

    At the heart of the Bible is a struggle. It is the story of a great dra-
ma in which humanity tries to keep in step with the heartbeat of love.
Occasionally God and his people walk in harmony, shoulder to shoulder
in sweet communion in the cool of the day. It was like this at the beginning
for Adam and his wife, given paradise to enjoy and guard. And there were
holy moments of great intimacy too, for Abram, Moses, Elijah, David,
Isaiah, John, and Peter. These were ordinary humans who felt the pull and
tug of the heartbeat of love upon their souls and responded to it. And yet

the struggle to hear and to heed God's voice was often lost by those very same people who, last week, had followed God's insistent call so carefully.

At times the struggle was lost by a whole nation, God's chosen nation, Israel, despite the pleas and warnings of the prophets, God's spokespeople, who bravely stood up in his name. "These people, whom I love to bless," announced God one day, "will be a vehicle for blessing to spread to the whole world. They are blessed, not because they are more loved, but simply so that others might, through them, discern and enjoy me too." God took these people, a ragtag collection of unknown tribes, and through an extraordinary tale of enslavement in Egypt, rescue, and deliverance across a harsh and forbidding desert, shaped them into a people that belonged to him. But alas, all too often, the blessing was kept to themselves and thereby it began to decay. The prophets came to call them out of their stupor and stubborn rebelliousness. "Trust," called out Jeremiah in the heat of political turmoil. To no avail. "Be merciful," declared Micah when the temptation was to be harsh and unyielding. But no one heard.

So it continued year after year, king after king, prophet after prophet until one day God's chosen people were taken away to a distant land—the land of Babylon—where they remained in exile, discarded and excluded for seventy years, in order that they might learn that mercy is better than . sacrifice and that love, for God and neighbor, is more important than anything else in the whole world. Those who heard the heartbeat and remembered from whence it came wrote down their struggles and heartaches, as well as their joys and times of jubilant thanksgiving. Their prayers and poems were collected together in the Psalms and became a treasured library.

And so God's time drew near. It was the time for his appearing, for his coming to his own people. He was called Emmanuel, God with us, or Jesus, God the Savior made flesh. He chose to come in disguise, as an infant in an unknown village to a simple peasant girl. He came to those who had lost their way, who had become deaf to the pulsing beat of love, who were blind to the yearning of God for them. He came to the forgotten people, the unimportant people, the people who lived each day in a place of shame and humiliation. This Jesus, God's own Son, would enter their own lostness to find them. He would even enter death for them, in order that they might know that in God's great drama, forgiveness, reconciliation, and a new beginning were available for all. When Jesus rose again after three days, everything became new. God's people were no longer those who simply named themselves, "Israel." Jesus had flung the doors of the kingdom of heaven open wide for all to enter. The community that gladly walked through those doors of welcome called themselves the "called out ones" or the "*ekklēsia*" or "the church" made up entirely of people. The remainder of the Bible concerns the struggle of this new community to understand itself, its relationship to Jesus, the carpenter from Nazareth who had come to reveal God to them and to tell them all about the heartbeat that never stops. It is an unfinished story . . .

Bmm . . . bmm . . . bmm . . . bmm.

Bibliography

Anderson, Gary. *Sin: A History*. New Haven: Yale University Press, 2009.

Appiah, Kwame Anthony. *The Honor Code: How Moral Revolutions Happen*. New York: Norton, 2010.

Bailey, Kenneth. *Poet and Peasant and Through Peasant Eyes: A Literary-Cultural Approach to the Parables in Luke*. Grand Rapids: Eerdmans, 1983.

———. *Jesus through Middle Eastern Eyes: Cultural Studies in the Gospels*. London: SPCK, 2008.

Barbeau, Jeffrey, editor. *Coleridge's Assertion of Religion: Essays on the Opus Maximum*. Leuven: Peeters, 2007.

Barth, Karl. *Church Dogmatics*. IV/1: *The Doctrine of Reconciliation*. Translated by G. W. Bromiley. Edited by G. W. Bromiley and T. F. Torrance. Edinburgh: T. & T. Clark, 1956.

Bonhoeffer, Dietrich. *Creation and Fall*. London: SCM, 1964.

———. *Ethics*. New York: Macmillan, 1955.

Botterwick, Johannes, and Rinngren, Helmer, eds. *Theological Dictionary of the Old Testament*, Vol. 2. Grand Rapids: Eerdmans, 1975.

Bowlby, John. *Attachment*. New York: Basic Books, 1983.

Brondos, David. *Paul on the Cross: Reconstructing the Apostle's Story of Redemption*. Minneapolis: Fortress, 2006.

Brueggemann, Walter. *Genesis*. Interpretation. Atlanta: John Knox. 1982.

———. *First and Second Samuel*. Interpretation. Atlanta: John Knox. 1990.

Clarke, N. "'We Live before the Faces of Others': To What Extent Can a Theology of the Face, and Facing, Serve the Cause of Reconciliation within our Contemporary World?" MLitt thesis, University of St. Andrews, 2009.

deSilva, David. *Despising Shame: Honor Discourse and Community Maintenance in the Epistle to the Hebrews*. Atlanta: Scholars, 1995.

———. *Honor, Patronage, Kinship and Purity: Unlocking New Testament Culture*. Downers Grove, IL: InterVarsity, 2000.

———. "Turning Shame into Honor: The Pastoral Strategy of 1 Peter." In *The Shame Factor: How Shame Shapes Society*, edited by Robert Jewett, 159–86. Eugene, OR: Cascade Books, 2011.

Erikson, Erik. *Identity and the Life Cycle*. New York: Norton, 1980.

Evans, Richard. *The Third Reich in Power*. New York: Penguin, 2005.

Bibliography

Ford, David. *Self and Salvation: Being Transformed.* Cambridge: Cambridge University Press, 1999.

————. *Shaping Theology: Engagements in a Religious and Secular World.* Oxford: Blackwell, 2007.

Ford, David, and Daniel Hardy. *Living in Praise: Worshipping and Knowing God.* Grand Rapids: Baker Academic, 2005.

Fowler, James. *Faithful Change: The Personal and Public Challenges of Postmodern Life.* Nashville: Abingdon, 1996.

————. *Weaving the New Creation: Stages of Faith and the Public Church.* San Fransisco: Harper, 1991.

Goldingay, John. *Psalms. Vol 3: Psalms 90–150.* Grand Rapids: Baker Academic, 2008.

Green, Joel, and Mark Baker. *Recovering the Scandal of the Cross.* Downers Grove, IL: InterVarsity, 2000.

Gunton, Colin. *The Actuality of the Atonement.* London: T. & T. Clark, 2003.

Hanson, K. C. "A Cultural Analysis of Matthew." *Semeia* 68 (1994) 81–111.

Hart, Trevor. "Redemption and Fall." In *The Cambridge Companion to Christian Doctrine,* edited by Colin Gunton, 189–206. Cambridge: Cambridge University Press, 1997.

Hengel, Martin. *Crucifixion.* Translated by John Bowden. London: SCM, 1977.

Jacobs, Alan. *Original Sin: A Cultural History.* London: SPCK, 2008.

Jenson, Matt. *The Gravity of Sin: Augustine, Luther, and Barth on Homo Incurvatus in Se.* London: T. & T. Clark, 2006.

Jenson, Robert. *Systematic Theology. Vol. 1. The Triune God.* Oxford: Oxford University Press, 1997.

Jewett, Robert. "Got Good Religion? Jesus and Paul on the Misuse of Piety to Earn Honor." In *The Shame Factor: How Shame Shapes Society,* edited by Robert K. Jewett, 187–208. Eugene, OR: Cascade Books, 2011.

————. *Romans: A Commentary.* Minneapolis: Fortress, 2006.

————. *Saint Paul Returns to the Movies.* Grand Rapids: Eerdmans, 1999.

Kavanagh, Patrick. *The Complete Poems.* Newbridge, UK: Goldsmith, 1988.

Keener, Craig. *A Commentary on the Gospel of Matthew.* Grand Rapids: Eerdmans, 1999.

Kelsey, David. *Eccentric Existence: A Theological Anthropology.* Louisville: Westminster John Knox, 2009.

Kraus, C. Norman. *Jesus Christ our Lord: Christology from a Disciple's Perspective.* Scottdale, PA: Herald, 1990.

Lawrence, Louise. *The Ethnography of the Gospel of Matthew: A Critical Assessment of the Use of the Honor and Shame Model in New Testament Studies.* Tübingen: Mohr Siebeck, 2003.

Lendon, J. E. *Empire of Honour: The Art of Government in the Roman World.* Oxford: Oxford University Press, 2002.

Lynd, Helen Merrell. *On Shame and the Search for Identity.* New York: Harcourt, Brace, 1958.

Malina, Bruce. *The Social Gospel of Jesus: The Kingdom of God in Mediterranean Perspective.* Minneapolis: Augsburg, 2000.

Malina, Bruce, and Richard Rohrbaugh. *Social-Science Commentary on the Gospel of John.* Minneapolis: Fortress, 1998.

Martinsen, Deborah. *Surprised by Shame: Dostoevsky's Liars and Narrative Exposure.* Columbus: Ohio State University, 2003.

Matthews, Victor. *More than Meets the Ear: Discovering the Hidden Contexts of Old Testament Conversations*. Grand Rapids: Eerdmans, 2008.

McFadyen, Alistair. *Bound to Sin: Abuse, Holocaust and the Christian Doctrine of Sin*. Cambridge: Cambridge University Press, 2000.

Moberly, Walter. *The Theology of the Book of Genesis*. Cambridge: Cambridge University Press, 2009.

Moltmann-Wendel, Elisabeth. *I Am My Body: A Theology of Embodiment*. New York: Continuum, 1995.

Neyrey, Jerome. "Honor and Shame in the Johannine Passion Narrative." *Semeia* 68 (1994) 113–37.

Pattison, Stephen. *Shame: Theory, Therapy, Theology*. Cambridge: Cambridge University Press, 2000.

Plantinga, Cornelius. *Not the Way It's Supposed to Be: A Breviary of Sin*. Grand Rapids: Eerdmans, 1995.

Rhoades, David. "Justification by Grace: Shame and Acceptance in a County Jail." In *The Shame Factor: How Shame Shapes Society*, edited by Robert K. Jewett, 86–102. Eugene, OR: Cascade Books, 2011.

Ricoeur, Paul. *Oneself as Another*. Translated by Kathleen Blamey. Chicago: University of Chicago Press, 1992.

Stansell, Gary. "Honor and Shame in the David Narratives." *Semeia* 68 (1994) 55–79.

Stiebert, Johanna. *The Construction of Shame in the Hebrew Bible*. JSOT 346. Sheffield, UK: Sheffield Academic Press, 2002.

Vanhoozer, Kevin. "The Atonement in Postmodernity: Guilt, Goats and Gifts." In *The Glory of the Atonement*, edited by Charles E. Hill and Frank A. James, 367–404. Downers Grove, IL: InterVarsity, 2004.

Volf, Miroslav. *Exclusion and Embrace: A Theological Exploration of Identity, Otherness and Reconciliation*. Nashville: Abingdon, 1996.

Wink, Walter. *Engaging the Powers: Discernment and Resistance in a World of Domination*. Minneapolis: Augsburg, 1992.

Witherington III, Ben. *Matthew*. Smyth and Helwys Bible Commentary. Macon, GA: Smyth & Helwys, 2006.

Wright, N. T. *Jesus and the Victory of God*. London: SPCK, 1996.

———. *What St. Paul Really Said*. Oxford: Lion, 1997.